Leading

The perfect collection of stories, jokes and wits of wisdom for leaders

By

Dan Spainhour

The Leadership Publishing Team

Winston Salem, North Carolina

www.leadershippublishingteam.com

Leading Narratives:

The perfect collection of stories, jokes and wits of wisdom for leaders

By

Dan Spainhour

ISBN-13: 978-0974856827

ISBN-10: 0974856827

The Leadership Publishing Team
Winston Salem, NC 27104

Introduction

Those who tell the stories rule the world.
--Hopi American Indian proverb

The most effective communicators have been great storytellers, from Aesop to Jesus to Abraham Lincoln to Mark Twain to Garrison Keillor. Why? Everyone loves a story. Stories are like windows to the truth. Leading through storytelling requires more than just spinning yarns; the stories must make important, relevant points. Through parables, Jesus imparted many of his most vital messages. Leaders need to appreciate this impact and prepare their own repertoire of parables that relate to their own particular enterprise.

—Adapted from Leadership Lessons of Jesus

A huge part of my coaching foundation was formed when as a very young coach, I got the opportunity to work the Duke Basketball Camp. My first year was the summer following Coach Mike Krzyzewski's third season at Duke which saw his team finish 11-17—his second consecutive losing season. At that time, there were lots of rumblings about how long it was going to be before he was fired. I'm sure Coach felt pressure but he never showed it. On the last night of camp we always had a pizza party with Coach K. We sat around talking hoops, discussed coaching philosophy and there was always the occasional BS story thrown in. I distinctly remember Coach K saying that coaching is as much about choosing words as it is about coaching strategies. He said you must know your team and you must tell vivid stories—stories that not only make people think but make them feel the way you want them to feel. Little did I know that I was receiving advice from an hall-of-fame coach who would go on to become a legend and the winningest college basketball coach ever.

I don't think it is a coincidence that the greatest leaders teach with stories. I think everyone needs a good story to tell and thanks to Coach K, I became very interested in learning what parables or interesting stories I could use to teach lessons to my team. Here are some I have collected from 34 years in the business. I will admit that some stories may be a little edgy and may not be considered "politically correct" by some but I chose to include all that I had in my collection. I hope no one is offended and that you enjoy them!

—Dan Spainhour, Winston Salem, NC

The Tale Of Two Wolves

A grandfather was discussing the ways of life with his grandson.

"There are two wolves that live in each of us. One is good, joyous, kind, compassionate and truthful. The other is not good, angry, selfish and evades the truth. These two wolves are in each of us and fight all the time."

The grandson had a troubled look on his face for a minute and then asked.

"Which wolf will win?"

The grandfather replied, "The one you feed."

Feed what you want more of and starve out things like negativity, self doubt and fear.

Wrong Email Address

A man was going on a tropical vacation with his wife. His wife was on a business trip so he went to the destination first and his wife would meet him there the next day.

When he reached his hotel, he decided to send his wife a quick email.

Unfortunately, when typing her address, he mistyped a letter and his note was directed instead to an elderly preacher's wife whose husband had passed away only the day before.

When the grieving widow checked her email, she took one look at the monitor, let out a piercing scream, and fell to the floor in a dead faint.

At the sound, her family rushed into the room and saw this note on the screen:

Dearest Wife,

Just got checked in. Everything prepared for your arrival tomorrow.

P.S. Sure is hot down here.

Not everything told to you is necessarily intended for you.

Will's Experience At The Airport

After his return from Rome, Will couldn't find his luggage in the airport baggage area. He went to the lost luggage office and told the woman there that his bags hadn't shown up on the carousel.

She smiled and told him not to worry because they were trained professionals and he was in good hands.

Then she asked Will, "Has your plane arrived yet?"

Even trained professionals have been known to ask dumb questions.

Mouthology

A professor was traveling by boat. On his way he asked the sailor who was on board:

"Do you know Biology, Ecology, Zoology, Geography, Physiology?

The sailor said no to all his questions.

Professor: "What the hell do you know? You will die of illiteracy."

After a while the boat started sinking. The sailor asked the Professor, do you know swiminology and escapology from sharkology?

The professor said no.

Sailor: "What the hell do you know? The sharkology and crocodilogy will eat your assology, headology and you will dieology because of your mouthology.

Condescending remarks always come back to bite you in the ass.

The Man Who Quits

The man who quits has a brain and a hand,

As good as the next, but lacks the sand,

That would make him stick, with a courage stout,

To whatever he tackles, and fight it out.

When in doubt—stick it out.

Captain

A navy captain is alerted by his first mate that there is a pirate ship coming towards their position. He asks a sailor to get him his red shirt.

The first mate asked the captain, "Why do you need a red shirt?"

The captain replies, "So that when I bleed, you guys don't notice and aren't discouraged."

The pirates board the boat and after a very hard battle the crew eventually are able to fight off the pirates.

The very next day, the captain is alerted that 50 more pirate ships are coming towards their boat. He yells, "Get me my brown pants!"

Being a quick thinking leader can help keep your mates hopeful.

Elephants

The class teacher asks students to name an animal that begins with an "E". One boy says, "Elephant."

Then the teacher asks for an animal that begins with a "T". The same boy says, "Two elephants."

The teacher becomes annoyed and sends the boy out of the class for being a smart aleck. After that she asks for an animal beginning with "M".

The boy shouts from the other side of the wall: "Maybe an elephant!"

Keep in mind there may be more than one right answer to any question you ask.

The Important Things In Life

A philosophy professor stood before his class with some items on the table in front of him. When the class began, wordlessly he picked up a very large and empty jar and proceeded to fill it with rocks, about 2 inches in diameter.

He then asked the students if the jar was full. They agreed that it was. So the professor then picked up a box of pebbles and poured them into the jar. He shook the jar lightly. The pebbles, of course, rolled into the open areas between the rocks.

He then asked the students again if the jar was full. They agreed it was. The professor picked up a box of sand and poured it into the jar. Of course, the sand filled up the remaining open areas of the jar.
He then asked once more if the jar was full. The students responded with a unanimous "Yes."

"Now," said the professor, "I want you to recognize that this jar represents your life. The rocks are the important things—your family, your partner, your health, your children—things that if everything else was lost and only they remained, your life would still be full. The pebbles are the other things that matter—like your job, your house, your car. The sand is everything else, the small stuff."

"If you put the sand into the jar first," he continued, "there is no room for the pebbles or the rocks. The same goes for your life. If you spend all your time and energy on the small stuff, you will never have room for the things that are important to you. Pay attention to the things that are critical to your happiness. Play with your children. Take your partner out dancing. There will always be time to go to work, clean the house, give a dinner party, or fix the disposal."

Take care of the rocks first – the things that really matter. Set your priorities. The rest is just sand.

I Have Learned...

I've learned...that you cannot make someone love you. All you can do is be someone who can be loved. The rest is up to them.

I've learned...that no matter how much I care, some people just don't care back.

I've learned...that it takes years to build up trust, and only seconds to destroy it.

I've learned...that no matter how good a friend is, they're going to hurt you every once in a while and you must forgive them for that.

I've learned...that it's not what you have in your life but who you have in your life that counts.

I've learned...that you should never ruin an apology with an excuse.

I've learned...that you can get by on charm for about fifteen minutes. After that, you had better know something.

I've learned...that you can do something in an instant that will give you heartache for life.

I've learned...that it's taking me a long time to become the person I want to be.

I've learned...that you should always leave loved ones with loving words.

I've learned...that you can keep going long after you think can't.

I've learned...that we are responsible for what we do, no matter how we feel.

I've learned...that either you control your attitude or it controls you.

I've learned...that regardless of how hot and steamy a relationship is at first, the passion fades and there had better be something else to take its place.

I've learned...that heroes are the people who do what has to be done when it needs to be done, regardless of the consequences.

I've learned...that money is a lousy way of keeping score.

I've learned...that my best friend and I can do anything or nothing and have the best time.

I've learned...that sometimes the people you expect to kick you when you're down will be the ones to help you get back up.

I've learned...that sometimes when I'm angry I have the right to be angry, but that doesn't give me the right to be cruel.

(Continued on page 10)

(Continued from page 9)

I've learned...that true friendship continues to grow, even over the longest distance. Same goes for true love.

I've learned...that just because someone doesn't love you the way you want them to doesn't mean they don't love you with all they have.

I've learned...that maturity has more to do with what types of experiences you've had and what you've learned from them and less to do with how many birthdays you've celebrated.

I've learned...that you should never tell a child their dreams are unlikely or outlandish. Few things are more humiliating, and what a tragedy it would be if they believed it.

I've learned...that your family won't always be there for you. It may seem funny, but people you aren't related to can take care of you and love you and teach you to trust people again. Families aren't biological.

I've learned...that it isn't always enough to be forgiven by others. Sometimes you have to learn to forgive yourself.

I've learned...that no matter how bad your heart is broken the world doesn't stop for your grief.

I've learned...that our background and circumstances may have influenced who we are, but we are responsible for who we become.

I've learned...that a rich person is not the one who has the most, but is one who needs the least.

I've learned...that just because two people argue, it doesn't mean they don't love each other. And just because they don't argue, it doesn't mean they do.

I've learned...that we don't have to change friends if we understand that friends change.

I've learned...that you shouldn't be so eager to find out a secret. It could change your life forever.

I've learned...that two people can look at the exact same thing and see something totally different.

I've learned...that no matter how you try to protect your children, they will eventually get hurt and you will hurt in the process.

I've learned...that even when you think you have no more to give, when a friend cries out to you, you will find the strength to help.

(Continued on page 11)

(Continued from page 10)

I've learned...that credentials on the wall do not make you a decent human being.

I've learned...that it's hard to determine where to draw the line between being nice and not hurting people's feelings, and standing up for what you believe.

I've learned...that people will forget what you said, and people will forget what you did, but people will never forget how you made them feel.

Great leaders never stop learning.

[handwritten note: Same for teachers in general. goes for people if you want to be great you can never stop learning]

The Coach . . .

I think that he shall never see,
A coach so good that never he
Does have to worry for his job,
Or try to please the supporting mob
Of fans and students and business men,
Who want the team to win again.
They have a ten-game winning streak
They lose but one—who is up the creek?
Though they had lost to a better team
It is the coach that's off the beam!

Ah, the life of a coach!

11

Little Eyes Upon You

There are little eyes upon you

and they're watching night and day.

There are little ears that quickly

take in every word you say.

There are little hands all eager

to do anything you do;

And a little boy who's dreaming

of the day he'll be like you.

You're the little fellow's idol,

you're the wisest of the wise.

In his little mind about you

no suspicions ever rise.

He believes in you devoutly,

holds all you say and do;

He will say and do, in your way

when he's grown up just like you.

There's a wide-eyed little fellow

who believes you're always right;

and his eyes are always opened,

and he watches day and night.

You are setting an example

every day in all you do;

For the little boy who's waiting

to grow up to be just like you.

Like it or not you are a role model.

12

How Poor Are We

One day a father, of a very wealthy family, took his son on a country with the firm purpose of showing his son how poor be. They spent a couple of days and nights on the farm of v be considered a very poor family.

On their return from the trip, the father asked his son, "How was the trip?" "It was great Dad!"

"Did you see how poor people can be?" the father asked. "Oh yeah," said the son.

"So what did you learn from the trip?" asked the father. The son answered, "I saw we have one dog and they have four. We have a pool that reaches to the middle of our garden and they have a creek that has no end. We have imported lanterns in our garden and they have the stars at night. Our patio reaches to the front yard and they have the whole horizon. We have a small piece of land to live on and they have fields that go beyond our sight. We have servants who serve us, but they serve others. We buy our food, but they grow theirs. We have walls around our property to protect us, they have friends to protect them." With this the boy's father was speechless.

Then his son added, "Thanks Dad for showing me how poor we are." *Everything is about perspective and your perspective may not be the same as those you are trying to influence.*

The Frog

A frog and his family had always lived in a small well and were quite content. The frog thought, life doesn't get any better than this. One day he looked up and noticed the light at the top of the well. He became curious, wondering what was up there. Against everyone's advice he climbed the side of the well and looked over the edge. What he saw was a pond. It was much bigger than the well! He ventured farther and discovered a huge lake. The well was a drop in the bucket compared to what was out there for him to enjoy.

Don't be afraid to step outside your comfort zone. Dare to dream bigger.

Everything I Need to Know About Life
I Learned From Noah's Ark

1. Plan ahead. It wasn't raining when Noah built the ark.

2. Stay fit. When you're 600 years old, someone might ask you to do something really big.

3. Don't listen to critics. Do what has to be done.

4. Build your future on the high ground.

5. For safety's sake, travel in pairs.

6. Two heads are better than one.

7. Speed isn't always an advantage. The cheetahs were on board, but so were the snails.

8. When you're stressed, float for a while.

9. Don't forget that we're all in the same boat.

10. When the shit gets really deep, don't sit there and complain— shovel!

11. Stay below deck during the storm.

12. Remember that the ark was built by amateurs and the Titanic was built by professionals.

13. Remember that the woodpeckers inside are often a bigger threat than the storm outside.

14. No matter how bleak it looks, there's always a rainbow on the other side.

15. Don't miss the boat.

Every story, every experience, every parable has lessons to be learned if you look for them.

The Eagle

A man found an eagle's egg and put it in the nest of a backyard hen. The eaglet hatched with the brood of chicks and grew up with them.

All his life the eagle did what the chickens did, thinking he was a chicken. He scratched the earth for worms and insects. He clucked and cackled. And he would thrash his wings and fly a few feet into the air.

Years passed and the eagle grew very old. One day he saw a magnificent bird far above him in the cloudless sky. It glided in graceful majesty among the wind currents, with scarcely a beat of its strong golden wings. The old eagle looked up in awe, "Who is that?" he asked. "That's the eagle, the king of the birds," said his neighbor. "He belongs to the sky. We belong to the earth—we're chickens."

So the eagle lived and died a chicken, for that's what he thought he was.

Be careful to not let those around you keep you from becoming what you were born to be.

Answer The Tough Questions

Little Billy asks his mother her age. She replies, "Gentlemen don't ask ladies that question." Billy then asks his mother how much she weighs. Again his mother replies, "Gentlemen don't ask ladies that question." The boy then asks, "Why did Daddy leave you?" To this, the mother says, "You shouldn't ask that," and sends him to his room.

On the way, Billy trips over his mother's purse. When he picks it up, her driver's license falls out. Billy runs back into the room.

"I know all about you now. You are 42 years old, weigh 138 pounds and Daddy left you because you got an 'F' in sex!"

Sometimes it best to answer the tough questions truthfully to keep others from making up their own answers.

A Team Of Geese

When you see geese heading south for the winter, flying in a "V" formation, you might consider what science has discovered as to why they fly that way. As each bird flaps its wings, it creates an uplift for the bird immediately following. By flying in a "V" formation, the whole flock adds at least 71 percent greater flying range than if each bird flew on its own.

Teams who share a common direction and sense of community can get where they are going more quickly and easily, because they are travelling on the thrust of one another. When a goose falls out of formation, it suddenly feels the drag and resistance of trying to go it alone and quickly gets back into formation to take advantage of the lifting power of the bird in front. When the head goose gets tired, it rotates back in the wing and another goose flies point. Geese honk from behind to encourage those up front to keep up their speed.

Finally, when a goose gets sick or is wounded, and falls out of the formation, two other geese fall out with that goose and follow it down to lend help and protection. They stay with the fallen goose until it is able to fly or until it dies; and only then do they launch out on their own, or with another formation to catch up with their own group.

If your team has the sense of a goose, it will stand by each other like that.

Feeling Good

A 60 year old woman is naked, jumping up and down on her bed laughing and singing. Her husband walks into the bedroom and sees her. He watches her awhile then says, "You look ridiculous, what on earth are you doing?" She says, "I just got my checkup and my doctor says I have the breasts of an eighteen-year-old."

She starts laughing and jumping again. He says, "Yeah, right. And what did he say about your 60 year-old ass?"

She says, "Well, your name never came up."

Off-handed remarks often come back at you.

16

The King And His Monkey

Once there was a king who had a pet monkey. This monkey was a fool, but was treated royally and moved freely in the king's palace. He was also allowed to enter the king's personal rooms that were forbidden even for the confidential servants.

One afternoon, the king was asleep, while the monkey kept a watch. All of a sudden, a fly came in the room and sat on the king's chest. The monkey swayed her away, but the fly would only go away for some time and return on the king's chest again.

The monkey got very angry and excited. The foolish monkey started chasing the fly witha a sword. As the fly sat on the king's chest again, the monkey drew his sword and hit the fly with all his might. The fly flew away unharmed, but the king was killed immediately.

The wise indeed say beware of a foolish friend. He can cause you more harm than your enemy.

The Frozen Bird

A little bird was flying south for the winter. It was so cold the bird froze and fell to the ground into a large field. While he was lying there, a cow came by and dropped some dung on him. As the frozen bird lay there in the pile of cow dung, he began to realize how warm he was. The dung was actually thawing him out. He lay there all warm and happy, and soon began sing for joy.

A passing cat heard the bird singing and came to investigate. Following the sound, the cat discovered the bird under the pile of cow dung, and promptly dug him out and ate him.

Morals of the story:
Not everyone who shits on you is your enemy.
Not everyone who gets you out of shit is your friend.
And when you're in deep shit, it's best to keep your mouth shut!

The Bathtub Test

Did you ever know that there is actually a test that can be given to you in a bathtub to see how sane you are? During a recent visit to a mental asylum, a guest asked the director, "How do you determine whether or not a patient should be institutionalized?"

"Well", said the director, "We fill up a bathtub, then we offer a teaspoon, a tea cup and a bucket to the patient and ask them to empty the bathtub."

"Oh, I see, so a normal person would use the bucket because it's bigger than the spoon or tea cup" the guest replied. "No", said the director, "a normal person would pull the plug. Do you want a bed near the window?"

The best solution may not always be one that is offered.

Two Bulls

There's a story of the two bulls, one young and full of enthusiasm, the other an older but wiser bull. They were both observing a herd of cows and the young bull says "let's charge down the hillside and have our wicked way with a couple of those cows." To which the older bull replies, "No, how about we stroll gently down the hillside and have our wicked way with them all."

How true it is that in our excitement, perhaps in anticipation of a quick win or to demonstrate our flare and prowess, we charge ahead confident of the outcome. When in fact, as it so often is, the slow and steady path leads to a more productive outcome, albeit not as dramatic at first. While we live in a world of fast food, instant coffee, speed dialing, microwave meals and express checkouts, it still pays to pause, slow down and ultimately achieve more than we can in our haste.

The Executive's Confidence

There was a business executive who was deep in debt and could see no way out. Creditors were closing in on him. Suppliers were demanding payment. He sat on a park bench, head in hands, wondering if anything could save his company from bankruptcy.

Suddenly an old man appeared before him. "I can see that something is troubling you," he said. After listening to the executive's woes, the old man said, "I believe I can help you." He asked the man his name, wrote out a check, and pushed it into his hand saying, "Take this money. Meet me here exactly one year from today, and you can pay me back at that time." Then he turned and disappeared as quickly as he had come.

The business executive saw in his hand a check for 500,000 dollars signed by John D. Rockefeller, then one of the richest men in the world! "I can erase my money worries in an instant!" he realized. But instead, the executive decided to put the uncashed check in his safe. Just knowing it was there might give him the strength to work out a way to save his business, he thought. With renewed optimism, he negotiated better deals and extended terms of payment. He closed several big sales. Within a few months, he was out of debt and making money once again.

Exactly one year later, he returned to the park with the uncashed check. At the agreed-upon time, the old man appeared. But just as the executive was about to hand back the check and share his success story, a nurse came running up and grabbed the old man. "I'm so glad I caught him!" she cried. "I hope he hasn't been bothering you. He's always escaping from the rest home and telling people he's John D. Rockefeller." And she led the old man away by the arm.

The astonished executive just stood there, stunned. All year long he'd been wheeling and dealing, buying and selling, convinced he had half a million dollars behind him.

He realized that it wasn't the money, real or imagined, that had turned his life around. It was his newfound self-confidence that gave him the power to achieve anything he went after.

Check Your Work

A store-owner overheard a boy talking on his phone:

Boy: "Maam, can you give me the job of cutting your lawn?"

Woman on phone: "I already have someone to cut my lawn."
Boy: "I will cut your lawn for half the price than the person who cuts your lawn now."

Woman: "I'm very satisfied with the person who is presently cutting my lawn."

Boy : *With more perseverance.* "I'll even sweep the floor and the stairs of your house for free."

Woman: "No, thank you."

With a smile on his face, he hung up. The store-owner, who was listening to all this, walked over to the boy. "Son, I like your attitude; I like that positive spirit and would like to offer you a job."

Boy: "No thanks." "But you were really pleading for one," the store owner said.

"No Sir, I was just checking my performance at the job I already have. I am the one who is working for that lady I was talking to!"

It's always a good idea to check up and see what your people think of the work you are doing before you find out the hard way.

The Farmer and His Sons

A father, being on the point of death, wanted to be sure that his sons would give the same attention to his farm as he himself had given it. He called them to his bedside and said, "My sons, there is a great treasure hidden in one of my vineyards." The sons, after his death, took their spades and mattocks and carefully dug over every portion of their land. They found no treasure, but the vines repaid their labor with an extraordinary and superabundant crop.

Motivate your people with what they think they want and you are in for a good return.

Bear Friends

Two men were traveling together, when a bear suddenly met them on their path. One of the men climbed up quickly into a tree and concealed himself in the branches. The other, seeing that he must be attacked, fell flat on the ground, and when the bear came up and felt him with his snout, and smelt him all over, he held his breath, and feigned the appearance of death as much as he could.

The bear soon left him, for it is said he will not touch a dead body. When he was quite gone, the other traveler descended from the tree, and jocularly inquired of his friend what it was the bear had whispered in his ear.

"He gave me this advice," his companion replied. "Never travel with a friend who deserts you at the approach of danger."

Misfortune always tests the sincerity of friends.

The Old Man's Pond

An elderly man in Louisiana owned a large farm for several years. He had a large pond in the back. It was properly shaped for swimming, so he fixed it up nice with picnic tables, horseshoe courts, and some apple trees. One evening the old farmer decided to go down to the pond, to look it over, as he hadn't been there for a while. Before he went, he grabbed a five-gallon bucket to bring back some apples. As he neared the pond, he heard voices shouting and laughing with glee. As he got closer, he saw it was a bunch of very pretty young women skinny-dipping in his pond. He made the women aware of his presence and they all went to the deep end.

One of the women shouted to him, "We're not coming out until you leave!" The old man replied, "I didn't come down here to watch you ladies swim naked or make you get out of the pond naked." Holding the bucket up, he said, "I'm here to feed the alligator!"

The ability to think quickly and on your feet often leads to unexpected rewards.

Danny helps the church lady

Little Danny comes home from Sunday school with a black eye. His father sees it and says, "Danny, how many times do I have to tell you not to fight with the other boys?" "But Dad, it wasn't my fault. We were all in church saying our prayers. We all stood up and my teacher in front of me had her dress stuck in the crack of her butt. I reached over and pulled it out. That's when she hit me!"

"Danny," the father said. "You don't do those kind of things to women." Sure enough, the very next Sunday Danny came home with the other eye black and blue. His father said, "Danny, I thought we had a talk!"

"But Dad," Danny said, "It wasn't my fault. There we were in church saying our prayers. We all stood up and my teacher in front of us had her dress in the crack of her butt again. Then Louie who was sitting next to me saw it and he reached over and pulled it out. Now I know she doesn't like this, so I pushed it back in!"

Clarity sounds simple, but many leaders struggle to speak with simplicity and often make assumptions that a message was clear.

The Turkey And The Bull

A turkey was chatting with a bull, "I would love to be able to get to the top of that tree," sighed the turkey, "but I haven't got the energy."

"Well, why don't you nibble on my droppings?" replied the bull. "They're packed with nutrients." The turkey pecked at a lump of dung and found that it gave him enough strength to reach the lowest branch of the tree.

The next day, after eating some more dung, he reached the second branch. Finally after a fourth night, there he was proudly perched at the top of the tree. Soon he was spotted by a farmer, who shot the turkey out of the tree.

Bottom line—Bullshit might get you to the top, but it wont keep you there.

The Bishop's Housekeeper

A bishop invited a young priest to dinner. During the meal, the priest noticed some signs of intimacy between the bishop and his housekeeper. As the priest was leaving, the bishop said to him quietly, "I can guess what you are thinking, but really our relationship is strictly proper."

A few days later the housekeeper remarked to the bishop that a valuable antique silver soup ladle was missing since the young priest's visit and she wondered if he had taken it. "I doubt it, but I will ask him," said the bishop.

So the bishop wrote to the priest:

Dear Father,
I am not saying that you did take a solid silver ladle from my house, and I am not saying that you did not take a silver ladle from my house, but the fact is that the ladle has been missing since your visit.

The bishop received the young priest's reply, which read:

Your Excellency,

I'm not saying that you do sleep with your housekeeper, and I'm not saying that you do not sleep with your housekeeper, but the fact is that if you were sleeping in your own bed, you would by now have found the ladle.

Accusations have a way of finding their way back to you.

Car Chaser

A farmer had a dog who used to sit by the roadside waiting for vehicles to come around. As soon as one came he would run down the road, barking and trying to overtake it. One day a neighbor asked the farmer, "Do you think your dog is ever going to catch a car?"

The farmer replied, "That is not what bothers me. What bothers me is what he would do if he ever caught one."

Do all you can to make sure that you and the people you are leading are not like a dog pursuing a meaningless goal.

The Exam

Four college friends had a party a couple hours away they really wanted to go to during the weekend before finals. They decided to go and ended up partying all weekend. They had a great time. After all the partying, they didn't make it back to school until Monday. Rather than taking the final then, they decided to find their professor after the final ended and explain to him why they missed it.

They explained that they had gone to the city for the weekend with the plan to come back and study but, unfortunately, they had a flat tire on the way back, didn't have a spare, and couldn't get help for a long time. As a result, they missed the final. The professor thought it over and then agreed they could make up the final the following day. The guys were elated and relieved. They studied that night and went in the next day at the time the professor had told them. He placed them in separate rooms and handed each of them a test booklet, and told them to begin. They looked at the first problem, worth 5 points. It was something simple about free radical formation. "Cool," they thought at the same time, each one in his separate room. "This is going to be easy." Each finished the problem and then turned the page. On the second page was written—for 95 points: Which tire?

Moral of the story? No matter how much you think you've covered your tracks there is always someone out there waiting to uncover them.

Dean's Wisdom

During a seminary faculty meeting, an angel suddenly appears and tells the Dean, "Sir, I will grant you whichever of three blessings you choose—wisdom, beauty or 10 million dollars."

For the Dean it was no contest. His theology is clear, and he happily choose wisdom. There was a flash of lightning, and the Dean appears transformed. But he just sits there, staring silently down at the table.

So one of his colleagues whispers to him, "why don't you test out your new found wisdom right away? Say something really wise to us."

The Dean sighs and says, "I should have taken the money."

Moral of the story—even though it is wise to learn from every decision the best time to ask for wisdom is before making a choice.

Organ Meeting

All the organs of the body were having a meeting, trying to decide who was in charge. The brain said: "I should be in charge, because I run all the body's systems, so without me nothing would happen."

"I should be in charge," said the heart, "because I pump the blood and circulate oxygen all over the body, so without me you'd all waste away."

"I should be in charge," said the stomach, "because I process food and give all of you energy."

"I should be in charge," said the rectum, "because I'm responsible for waste removal."

All the other body parts laughed at the rectum and insulted him, so in a huff, he shut down tight. Within a few days, the brain had a terrible headache, the stomach was bloated, and the blood was toxic. Eventually the other organs gave in. They all agreed that the rectum should be the boss.

The moral of the story? No matter how important you think you are there's probably some asshole really controlling things.

The Hedgehogs

It was the coldest winter ever. Many animals died because of the cold. The hedgehogs, realizing the situation, decided to group together to keep warm. This way they covered and protected themselves but the quills of each one wounded their closest companions.

After awhile, they decided to distance themselves one from the other and they began to die, alone and frozen. So they had to make a choice: either accept the quills of their companions or disappear from the Earth.

Wisely, they decided to go back to being together. They learned to live with the little wounds caused by the close relationship with their companions in order to receive the heat that came from the others. This way they were able to survive.

The best relationship is not the one that brings together perfect people, but when each individual learns to live with the imperfections of others and can admire the other person's good qualities.

Socrates Three Filter Test

An acquaintance met the great philosopher Socrates and said, "Do you know what I just heard about your friend?"

Wait a minute," Socrates replied. "Before you talk to me about my friend, take a moment to use the triple filter test on what you're going to say. The first filter is Truth. Have you made absolutely sure that what you are about to tell me is true?"

"Well, no," the man said, "actually I just heard about it and.." "Ok," said Socrates. "So you don't really know if it's true or not. Try the second filter, the filter of Goodness. Is what you are about to tell me about my friend something good?"

"Umm, no, on the contrary..." " So," Socrates said, "you want to tell me something bad about my friend, but you're not certain it's true. There's one filter left—the filter of Usefulness. Is what you want to tell me about my friend going to be useful to me?" "No, not really."

"Well," concluded Socrates, "if what you want to tell me is neither true, nor good, nor even useful, why tell it to me at all?"

Just as important as not spreading gossip is having the fortitude not to listen to it as well.

The Professor's Glass

A professor began his class by holding up a glass with some water in it. He held it up for all to see and asked the class "How much do you think this glass weighs?"

"Not much" the students answered. "My question is what would happen if I held it up like this for a few minutes?"

"Nothing" the students said. "Ok what would happen if I held it up like this for an hour?" the professor asked. "Your arm would begin to ache" said the students.

"You're right, now what would happen if I held it for a day?" "Your arm could go numb; you might have severe muscle stress and paralysis" said another student and all the students laughed.

"Very good. But during all this, did the weight of the glass change?" "No.""Then what caused the arm ache and the muscle stress?" The students were puzzled.

"What should I do now to stop the pain?" asked professor. "Put the glass down!" said the students. "Exactly!"

Life's problems are something like this. Hold it for a few minutes and they seem ok. Think of them for a long time and they begin to ache. Hold it even longer and they begin to paralyze you. It is important to think of the challenges in your life, but even more important is to put them down at the end of every day before you go to sleep. That way, you are not stressed, you wake up every day fresh and can handle any challenge that comes your way. When you start each day, remember to put the glass down!

Nickel and Dimed

Little Johnny is always being teased by the other neighborhood boys for being stupid. Their favorite joke is to offer Johnny his choice between a nickel and a dime—little Johnny always takes the nickel.

One day, after Johnny takes the nickel, a neighbor takes him aside and says, "Johnny, those boys are making fun of you. Don't you know that a dime is worth more than a nickel, even though the nickel's bigger?"

Johnny grins and says, "Well, if I took the dime, they'd stop doing it, and so far I've made 20 dollars!"

Sometimes people are smarter than their actions appear.

The Lumberjack

A very strong woodcutter asked for a job as a lumberjack and he got it. The pay was really good and so were the work conditions. For those reasons, the woodcutter was determined to do his best.

His boss gave him an axe and showed him the area where he was to work. The first day, the woodcutter brought back 18 trees. "Congratulations," his boss said. "Keep up the good work!" Motivated by his boss's words, the woodcutter tried harder the next day, but could only bring 15 trees. The third day he tried even harder, but could only bring 10 trees.

Day after day he was bringing less and less trees. "I must be losing my strength," he thought. He went to the boss and apologized, saying that he could not understand what was going on.

"When was the last time you sharpened your axe?" the boss asked. "Sharpen? I had no time to sharpen my axe. I have been very busy trying to cut trees."

We all need time to relax, to think and meditate, to learn and grow. If we don't take the time to sharpen the "axe", we will become dull and lose our effectiveness.

The Drunk Sailor

There was a sailor who worked on the same boat for three years. One night he got drunk. This was the first time it ever happened. The captain recorded it in the log, "The sailor was drunk tonight." The sailor read it, and he knew this comment would affect his career, so he went to the captain, apologized and asked the captain to add that it only happened once in three years which was the complete truth.

The captain refused and said, "What I have written in the log is the truth." The next day it was the sailor's turn to fill in the log. He wrote, "The captain was sober tonight." The captain read the comment and asked the sailor to change or add to it explaining the complete truth because this implied that the captain was drunk every other night. The sailor told the captain that what he had written in the log was the truth.

Although both statements were true they conveyed misleading messages.

Conductor Andy

Andy was in the kitchen playing with his toy train as his father cooked dinner. Andy stopped the train and said, "All you assholes who want to get off, get the hell off. All those who want to get on, get the hell on!"

"Andy!" exclaimed his father. "I can't believe you are using that language! You should be ashamed of yourself! I want you to go to your room and don't come back until you have thought about what you've done!"

So Andy goes to his room and comes back an hour or so later. He resumes playing with his train, only this time when he stops it he says, "All of you ladies and gentlemen who want to get off, you may now get off, and those who want to get on, you may now also get on. And as for those of you who have a problem with the hour delay, talk to the asshole in the kitchen!"

Moral? Sending a problem away doesn't fix it. Sometimes it comes back pointed at you!

The Priest And The Nun

A very pretty nun was in town and needed a ride back to the convent A priest came along and offered her a ride. She got in and crossed her legs, forcing her gown to reveal a leg. The priest nearly had an accident. After controlling the car, he stealthily slid his hand up her leg.

The nun said, "Father, remember Psalm 129?" The priest removed his hand. But, while changing gears, he let his hand slide up her leg again. The nun once again said, "Father, remember Psalm 129?"

The priest apologized, "Sorry sister but the flesh is weak."

Arriving at the convent, the nun went on her way. On his arrival at the church, the priest rushed to look up Psalm 129.

It said, "Go forth and seek, further up, you will find glory."

If you are not well informed in your job, you might miss a great opportunity!

Noble's Prize

About a hundred years ago, a man looked at the morning newspaper and to his surprise and horror, read his name in the obituary column. The newspapers had reported the death of the wrong person by mistake. His first response was shock. Am I here or there?

When he regained his composure, his second thought was to find out what people had said about him. The obituary read, "Dynamite King Dies." And also "He was the merchant of death." This man was the inventor of dynamite and when he read the words "merchant of death," he asked himself a question, "Is this how I am going to be remembered?"

He got in touch with his feelings and decided that this was not the way he wanted to be remembered. From that day on, he started working toward peace. His name was Alfred Nobel and he is remembered today by the great Nobel Peace Prize.

Just as Alfred Nobel got in touch with his feelings and redefined his values, we should all step back and do the same.

The Angry Wife

An angry wife met her husband at the door. There was alcohol on his breath and lipstick on his collar.

"I assume," she snarled, "that there is a very good reason for you to come waltzing in here at six o'clock in the morning?"

"There is,"he replied. "Breakfast!"

No matter how certain of another's reasoning or motives you can never assume what their answer will be.

Sitting Around

A crow was sitting on a tree, doing nothing all day. A rabbit asked him, "Can I also sit like you and do nothing all day long?" The crow answered: "Sure, why not."

So, the rabbit sat on the ground below the crow, and rested. A fox jumped on the rabbit and ate it.

Moral of the story—to be sitting and doing nothing, you must be sitting very high up!

The Pop Quiz

During Mark's first month of college, the professor gave his students a pop quiz. He was a conscientious student and had breezed through the questions, until he read the last one: "What is the first name of the woman who cleans the school?" Surely this was some kind of joke. He had seen the cleaning woman several times. She was tall, dark-haired and in her 50s, but how would he know her name?

He handed in his paper, leaving the last question blank. One student asked if the last question would count toward the quiz grade.

"Absolutely," said the professor. "In your careers, you will meet many people. All are significant. They each deserve your attention and care, even if all you do is smile and say 'hello'". Mark never forgot that lesson and he learned her name was Dorothy.

Nothing sounds sweeter to a person than their own name.

The Fisherman And The Snake

A fisherman observed a snake swimming towards his boat. When the snake reached the boat the fisherman could see that he had a frog in his mouth. Feeling sorry for the frog he reached down and carefully removed the frog from the snake's mouth and set it free.

But then, feeling sorry for the snake he looked around to see what he could give him. He found a bottle of bourbon, poured a capful and gave it to the snake. The snake then swam away. The fisherman was feeling content from his good deeds when about ten minutes later he heard a knocking at the side of the boat. When he looked over the side he saw the snake had returned this time with two frogs in his mouth.

Good deeds without proper explanation may lead to entitlement.

Face Freeze

Finding one of her students making faces at others on the playground, Mrs. Smith stopped to gently reprimand the child. Smiling sweetly, the teacher said, "Davey, when I was a little girl, I was told if that I made ugly faces, it would freeze and it would stay like that."

Little Davey looked up and replied, "Well, Ms. Smith, you can't say you weren't warned."

Trying to change behavior with false statements is never a good idea and often ends up making you look bad.

Three Birds on a Wire

A teacher was helping her students with a math problem. One boy in particular was having difficult time so, she recited the following story, "Evan, there are three birds sitting on a telephone wire. A man with a gun shoots one of the birds. How many birds are left on the wire?" The boy pauses. "None," he replied thoughtfully.

"No, no, no. Let's try again, maybe you didn't hear me correctly," the teacher says patiently. She holds up three fingers. "There are three birds sitting on a wire. A man with a gun shoots one," she puts down one finger, "how many birds are left on the wire?"

"None," the boy says with authority. The teacher sighs. "Tell me how you came up with that." "It's simple," says the boy, "after the man shot one bird, the noise from the gun scared the other two away."

"Well," she says, "that's not technically correct, but I like the way you think." "Thanks," chimes the boy, "now let me ask you a question."

"Okay," she said guardedly. "There are three women sitting on a bench eating popsicles. One woman is licking the popsicle, one woman is biting the popsicle, and one is sucking the popsicle. Which one is married?" he asked innocently.

The teacher looked at the boy's angelic face and writhed in agony, turning three shades of red. "C'mon," the boy said impatiently, "which one is it, the one licking the popsicle, the one biting it, or the one sucking it? Which one is married?"

"Well, uh," she gulped and in a barely audible whisper replied, "the one who's sucking?"

"No," he says with surprise, "the one with the wedding ring. But I like the way you think."

Moral? Before you agree to answer make sure you are comfortable with the question.

Square Balls

A little old lady went into the headquarters of the Bank of America one day, carrying a large bag of money. She insisted that she must speak with the president of the bank to open a savings account because, "It's a lot of money!"

The receptionist objected, stating, "You can't just walk in here and expect to see the president of the Bank. He's a very busy man." "But I am here to make a very large cash deposit," added the old woman.

The receptionist momentarily looked at the sack of money, then walked back to one of the rear offices. She came back and said, "You're in luck this morning, he will see you," and ushered her in to see the president of the Bank. When she walked into a large office she saw a nicely tailored man behind a great oaken desk. The bank president stood up and asked, "How can I help you?"

She replied, "I would like to open a savings account," and placed the bag of money on his desk. "How much would you like to deposit?" he asked curiously. "180,000, if you please," and dumped the cash out of her bag onto his desk.

The president was surprised to see all this cash, so he asked her, "Ma'am, I'm surprised you're carrying so much cash around, especially a woman at your stage in life. Where did you come by this kind of money?" The old lady coyly replied, "I make bets."

Surprised, the president then asked, "Bets? What kind of bets?" The old woman said, "Well, for example, I'll bet you 25,000 dollars that your balls are square."

"What?!" cried the man, "you want to bet me 25,000 dollars that my balls, my testicles, are square?" He could hardly hold back from laughing. "Yes, you heard me. In fact, by ten o'clock tomorrow morning, I'll bet you 25,000 dollars that your balls will be square."

The man smiled broadly, thinking he had a live one. "You've got yourself a bet!" and shook her hand. The little old lady then said, "Okay, but since there is a lot of money involved, may I bring my lawyer with me tomorrow at 10:00 a.m. as a witness?" "Sure!" replied the confident president.

That night, the president got very nervous about the bet and spent a long time in front of a mirror checking his balls, turning from side to side, again and again. He thoroughly checked them out until he was sure that there was absolutely no way his balls were square and that he would win the bet.

The next morning, at precisely 10:00 a.m., the little old lady appeared

(Continued on page 34)

(Continued from page 33)

with her lawyer at the president's office. She introduced the lawyer to the president and repeated the bet— "25,000 dollars says the president's balls are square!"

The president agreed with the bet again and the old lady asked him to drop his pants so they could all see. The president was concerned about bearing his privates for all to see but knew this was the only way to win bet. So he dropped his pants. The little old lady peered closely at his balls and then asked if she could feel them.

"Well, Okay," said the president, obviously embarrassed. Thinking to himself, "25,000 dollars is a lot of money, I guess it's okay." He then said, "Yes, 25,000 dollars is a lot of money, so I guess you should be absolutely sure."

As the old woman started to feel the banker's testicles, he noticed that the lawyer was quietly banging his head against the wall. The president asked the old lady, "What the hell's the matter with your lawyer?"

The old lady replied, "Nothing, except I bet him 100,000 dollars that at 10:00 a.m. today, I'd have the balls of the Bank's President in my hands."

Always remember don't doubt what people say they will do just because your limited view doesn't see anyway they can.

The Little Piano Player

A man walks into a bar and sees his friend sitting beside a 12-inch person playing a piano. He says to his friend, "That's amazing. How in the world did you get that?"

The man pulls out a bottle and tells him to rub it and make a wish. He rubs the bottle, and a puff of smoke pops out. A genie appears and tells him that he can have one wish. So the man thinks and says, "I wish I had a million bucks." The genie says, "OK, go outside, and your wish will be granted."

The man goes outside, but all he finds are ducks everywhere—filling the sky and roads. He goes back in and tells his friend what happened, and his friend replies, "I know, I know. Did you really think I wanted a 12-inch pianist?"

Moral—Not only must you make your instructions very clear—you must also ensure that your people are very clear about what it is you want done.

The Mailman's Last Day

It was the mailman's last day on the job after 35 years of carrying the mail through all kinds of weather to the same neighborhood. When he arrived at the first house on his route he was greeted by the whole family there, who congratulated him and sent him on his way with a big gift envelope.

At the second house they presented him with a box of fine cigars. The folks at the third house handed him a selection of terrific fishing lures. At the next house he was met at the door by a strikingly beautiful woman in a revealing negligee. She took him by the hand, gently led him through the door, closed it behind him and led him up the stairs to the bedroom where she blew his mind with the most passionate lovemaking he had ever experienced.

He fell asleep and when he woke up he went downstairs, where she had fixed him a giant breakfast—eggs, potatoes, ham, sausage, blueberry waffles, and fresh-squeezed orange juice. When he was truly satisfied she poured him a cup of steaming coffee. As she was pouring, he noticed a dollar bill sticking out from under the cup's bottom edge.

"All this was just too wonderful for words," he said, "but what's the dollar bill for?" "Well," she said, "a couple of days ago, I told my husband that yesterday would be your last day, and that we should do something special for you. I asked him what to give you."

He said, "Screw him, give him a dollar." The lady then said, "The breakfast was my idea."

What you mean and what is interpreted is often two very different things.

The Sound of the Forest

Back in the third century A.D., the King sent his son, the Prince, to the temple to study under a great master. Because the Prince was to succeed his father as king, the master was to teach the boy the basics of being a good ruler. When the prince arrived at the temple, the master sent him to be alone to the forest. After one year, the prince was to return to the temple to describe the sound of the forest.

When prince returned, the master asked the boy to describe all that he could hear. "Master," replied the prince, "I could hear the cuckoos sing, the leaves rustle, the hummingbirds hum, the crickets chirp, the grass blow, the bees buzz, and the wind whisper and holler." When the prince had finished, the master told him to go back to the forest to listen to what more he could hear. The prince was puzzled by the master's request. Had he not discerned every sound already?

For days and nights on end, the young prince sat alone in the forest listening. But he heard no sounds other than those he had already heard. Then one morning, as the prince sat silently beneath the trees, he started to discern faint sounds unlike those he had ever heard before. The more acutely he listened, the clearer the sounds became. The feeling of enlightenment enveloped the boy. "These must be the sounds the master wished me to discern," he reflected.

When the prince returned to the temple, the master asked him what more he had heard. "Master," responded the prince reverently, "when I listened most closely, I could hear the unheard—the sound of flowers opening, the sound of the sun warming the earth, and the sound of the grass drinking the morning dew." The master nodded approvingly. "To hear the unheard," remarked the master "is a necessary discipline to be a good ruler.

Only when a leader has learned to listen closely to people's hearts, hearing feelings they don't communicate, pains unexpressed, and complaints not spoken of, can he hope to inspire confidence in his people, understand when something is wrong, and meet the true needs of his citizens. The demise comes when leaders listen only to superficial words and do not penetrate deeply into the souls of the people to hear their true opinions, feelings, and desires.

Perhaps

Once upon a time there was an old farmer who had worked his crops for many years. One day his horse ran away. Upon hearing the news, his neighbors came to visit. "Such bad luck," they said sympathetically.

"Perhaps," the farmer replied.

The next morning the horse returned, bringing with it three other wild horses. "What great luck!" the neighbors exclaimed.

"Perhaps," replied the old man.

The following day, his son tried—to ride one of the untamed horses, was thrown, and broke his leg. The neighbors again came to offer their sympathy on his misfortune.

"Perhaps," answered the farmer.

The day after, military officials came to the village to draft young men into the army. Seeing that the son's leg was broken, they passed him by. The neighbors congratulated the farmer on how well things had turned out.

"Perhaps," said the farmer.

Good leaders never get too worked up about things or situations—be they good or bad.

Eleanor's response

On April 12th, 1945, Vice-President Harry Truman was summoned to the White House. Ushered into Eleanor Roosevelt's sitting room, the vice president was gently informed that President Roosevelt had died.

After a moment's reflection, "Is there anything I can do for you?" Truman asked Eleanor. Mrs. Roosevelt replied. "You're the one in trouble now!"

What appears to be a difficult time for someone may actually be a relief.

I'd Rather Be a Happy Turtle

Zi was a brilliant philosopher and strategist who lived in ancient China. His abilities were many and several rulers sought his services. One of them, King Wei, sent his courtiers out to Zi's pastoral home to invite him to come to Wei's court and be the leader's chief counselor. They found Zi fishing by the river bank.

Seeing his poor situation, they thought Zi would jump at the chance for status and reward. Yet when they made their proposal to him, he said, "Once upon a time there was a sacred turtle, which was happy living his life in the mud. Yet, because he was sacred, the king's men found him, took him to the royal palace, killed him and used his shell to foresee the future. Now tell me, would that turtle prefer to have given up his life to be honored at the palace, or would he rather be alive and enjoying himself in the mud?"

The courtiers responded that, of course, the turtle would be happier in the mud. To which Zhuang Zi replied, "And so you have my answer. Go home and let me be a happy turtle here in the mud."

Never assume that you know what is best for another person.

Brother Leo

A legend tells of a French monastery known throughout Europe for the extraordinary leadership of a man known only as Brother Leo. Several monks began a pilgrimage to visit Brother Leo to learn from him. Almost immediately, they began to bicker about who should do various chores.

On the third day they met another monk going to the monastery, and he joined them. This monk never complained or shirked a duty, and whenever the others would fight over a chore, he would gracefully volunteer and do it himself. By the last day, the others were following his example, and from then on they worked together smoothly.

When they reached the monastery and asked to see Brother Leo, the man who greeted them laughed. "But our brother is among you!" And he pointed to the fellow who had joined them.

A great leader earns his reputation through his deeds not through his reputation.

King's Diamond

Once upon a time, a long time ago, there was a king in Ireland. Ireland had lots of small kingdoms in those days, and this king's kingdom was one among many. Both the king and the kingdom were quite ordinary and nobody paid much attention to either of them.

But one day, the king received a huge beautiful diamond from a relative who had died. It was the largest diamond anyone had ever seen. It dazzled everyone. The other kings began to pay attention to him for if he had a diamond like this he must be special. The people, too, came from far and wide to see the diamond. The king had it on constant display in a glass box so that all who wished could come to see and admire it. Of course, armed guards kept a constant vigil. Both king and kingdom prospered, and the king attributed all his good fortune to the diamond.

One day a nervous guard asked to see him. The guard was visibly shaken. He told the king terrible news—the diamond had developed a flaw. A crack right down the middle. The king was horrified and ran to the glass box to see for himself. It was true. The diamond was now flawed terribly.

He called all the jewelers in the land to ask their advice. They gave him only bad news. The flaw was so deep, they said, that if they were to try to sand it down, they would grind it to practically nothing, and if they tried to split it into two still substantial stones, it easily might shatter into a million fragments.

As the king was pondering these terrible options, an old jeweler who had arrived late came to him and said, 'If you will give me a week with that stone, I think I can fix it."' The king didn't believe him at first because the other jewelers were so sure it couldn't be fixed, but the old man was insistent. Finally the king relented, but said he couldn't let the diamond out of his castle. The old man said that would be all right. He could work there and the guards could stand outside the room where he was working.

The king, having no better solution, agreed to let the old man work. For a week he and the guards hovered about, hearing scratching and gentle pounding and grinding. They wondered what he was doing and what would happen if the old man were tricking them.

Finally, the week was up and the old man came out of the room. King and guards rushed in to see the old man's work, and the king burst into tears of joy. It was better! The old man had carved a perfect rose on the top of the diamond, and the crack that ran down inside now was the stem of the rose.

(Continued on page 40)

(Continued from page 39)

Every leader has a special gift visible for all to see and even admire. Effective and genuine leadership, however, does not deny fault and flaw in self, pretending perfection and fueling delusions of righteousness. A good leader does not hide their weakness, which is the other side of the gift, but confesses it unabashedly.

A good leader grants permission to self and others for the work of transformation, turning the very weakness into its corresponding strength: fear to courage, pride to self-respect, perfectionism to patience, anger to generosity, etc.

Finally, a good leader is not embarrassed by the process of healing. By being openly vulnerable to another's healing and help, the good leader allows something beautiful and unexpected to emerge out of the flaw. A rose grows with the thorn.

The Drunk And The Alligator

A guy walks into a bar with an alligator. It's about 10 feet long. The bartender flips out and says, "Hey buddy, you gotta get that son of a bitch outta here. It's going to bite one of my customers and I'm going to get sued."

The guy says, "No no no, it's a tame alligator. I'll prove it to you." He picks up the alligator and puts it on the bar. Then he unzips his pants, pulls out his package and sticks it in the alligator's mouth. The alligator just keeps his mouth open. After about 5 minutes, he pulls it out of the alligator's mouth and zips up his pants and says, "See, I told you it was a tame alligator. Anybody else want to try it?"

The drunk down at the end of the bar says, "Yeah, I'd like to try it but I don't think I can hold my mouth open that long"

People often see things from very different perspectives.

The Pencil

A long time ago a master pencil maker was preparing to put a very important pencil into this beautiful handcrafted box but before doing so he took the pencil aside to give it some words of encouragement. He said, "Listen pencil, there are five things that you really need to know. If you can remember these five things you're going to become the best damn pencil that you can possibly be. You are going to have a huge impact on the world."

"First," he said, "You'll be able to do lots of great things but only if you allow yourself to be held in someone else's hands."

"Second," he said, "Sharpening is going to be very painful but it's vital if you want to become a great pencil."

"Third," he said, "Because you have an eraser, you'll be able to correct most of your mistakes but honestly, there are going to be some mistakes that are going to be harder to erase than others."

"Four, you may or may not look on the outside like you're a great pencil but remember it's what's on the inside that's most important. In fact, it's the inside of you that's the most important of all.

"Fifth, whatever surface it is that you write on, whether it's soft or hard, rough or not, you've got to leave your mark so just keep on writing."

In order to make your mark follow the attributes of the pencil.

Lessons from a Crack Pot

There was an elderly woman who had the responsibility of gathering water for her family each day. Because the family lived in a very remote and dry region, she had to walk far to get the water. She could only carry two pots at a time and so, needed to make the trip every day.

The elderly woman did not have the means for new materials. As a result, only one pot was in perfect working order. The other pot had a crack running half way down the side. The first was the envy of the latter. Making matters worse, the whole pot often belittled the other, critiquing it of lacking performance: "You are a sorry excuse for a pot! Every day you lose half your water. I will give you a poor performance review. You're not even meeting half of your objectives and you are draining our resources. You need to be replaced."

Of course, these negative remarks wore on the cracked pot. Over time, the poor pot began to believe the negative feedback about itself. Until, one day, the cracked pot nearly gave up and apologized to the elderly woman, asking to be replaced: "My lady, I am so sorry for failing you. Every day, we walk to and from the well and I can not hold on to all the water you place in me. I am a poor performer. You must be awfully disappointed in me. Please, replace me with another, newer model, so you can be more successful!"

Upon hearing this, the lady gasped. She now realized the cracked pot did not fully understand its role. "But, cracked pot, you provide so many benefits to me and our family that you do not realize. Haven't you noticed all the flowers and vegetables growing up on your side of the path? I knew you dripped water and so I planted seeds along your side of our path. Your water nurtured those plants and vegetables. I picked the flowers to make our home beautiful and the vegetables to feed our family. The other pot may seem more complete, but I would have to stop and tip it every time I wanted to give the plants a drink. In contrast, water flows from you perfectly—at a consistent and steady pace."

Every team member has a role to play and what is often looked upon as weakness can actually be a strength.

Big people do small things

Over 200 years ago, a man in civilian clothes rode past a small group of tired and battled weary soldiers. They were digging what appeared to be an important defensive position.

The leader of the group wasn't making any effort to help. He just shouted orders and threatened to punish the group if the work wasn't completed within the hour.

"Why aren't you helping?" the stranger asked on horseback. "I'm in charge! The men do as I tell them," said the leader. He added "Help them yourself if you feel so strongly about it." To the mean leader's surprise the stranger got off his horse and helped the men until the job was finished.

Before he left the stranger congratulated the men for their work, and approached the confused leader. "You should notify top command next time your rank prevents you from supporting your men and I will provide a more permanent solution," the stranger said. Up close, the now humbled leader recognized General George Washington and was taught a lesson he would never forget.

How high you sit on your horse doesn't decide the quality of your leadership.

The Disappearing Dinner Guest

A man and a woman were having dinner in a fine restaurant. Their waitress, taking another order at a table a few paces away noticed that the man was slowly sliding down his chair and under the table, with the woman acting unconcerned. The waitress watched as the man slid all the way down his chair and out of sight under the table. Still, the woman dining across from him appeared calm and unruffled, apparently unaware that her dining companion had disappeared.

After the waitress finished taking the order, she came over to the table and said to the woman, "Pardon me, ma'am, but I think your husband just slid under the table."

The woman calmly looked up at her and replied firmly, "No he didn't. He just walked in the door."

Moral—Always keep in mind that things may not be what they appear to be.

A Leader's Impact

In September of 1862, the civil war tilted decisively in favor of the south. The morale of the northern army dipped to its lowest point of the war. Large numbers of Union troops were in full retreat in Virginia. Northern leaders began to fear the worst. They saw no way to reverse the situation and turn the beaten, exhausted troops into a useful army again.

There was only one general with the ability to work such a miracle. That was General George McClellan. He had trained the men for combat and they admired him. But neither the war department nor the rest of the cabinet members saw this connection. Only president Abraham Lincoln recognized General McClellan's leadership skills.

Fortunately, Lincoln ignored the protests of his advisors and reinstated McClellan back in command. He told the general to go down to Virginia and give those soldiers something no other man on earth could give them—enthusiasm, strength and hope. McClellan accepted the command. He mounted his great black horse and cantered down the dusty Virginia roads.

What happened next is hard to describe. Northern leaders couldn't explain it. Union soldier couldn't explain it either. Even McClellan couldn't quite explain what happened. General McClellan met the retreating Union columns, waved his cap in the air and shouted words of encouragement. When the worn out men saw their beloved teacher and leader, they began to take heart once again. They were moved with an unshakable feeling that now things could be different, that finally things could be all right again.

Bruce Catton, the great civil war historian, describes this excitement that grew when word spread that McClellan was back in command. "Down mile after mile of Virginia roads the stumbling column came alive. Men threw their caps and knapsacks into the air, and yelled until they could yell no more because they saw this dapper little rider outlined against the purple starlight."

And this, in a way, was the turning point of the war. No one could ever quite explain how it happened. But whatever it was, it gave President Lincoln and the north what was needed. And history was forever changed because of it.

This story illustrates dramatically the impact a leader can have on the human spirit.

Don't Rest on Your Laurels

One day a field marshal requested an audience with the great leader Napoleon, and Napoleon knew what was coming. But as every good leader must, Napoleon agreed to hear him out. The field marshal brought news of a great victory he had achieved. He talked for a long time about his accomplishment, piling detail upon detail.

Napoleon listened closely throughout the entire narration, but said nothing. The officer was disappointed. He had hoped for a more enthusiastic reception, as well as Napoleon's congratulations. Neither was forthcoming.

Summing up, the marshal repeated much of what he had already stated. As the officer rambled on, Napoleon continued to listen politely, and the marshal interpreted this as encouragement. Surely, he thought, Napoleon will now give me the praise I so richly deserve.

When the marshal finally stopped talking, Napoleon asked him one question: "What did you do the next day?"

A great leader never rests on his laurels and leaves it to others to bestow praise on them.

The Flagpole

A boy offered a girl 10 dollars to climb a flagpole. The girl agreed and climbed the flagpole. When she gets home she tells her mother what happened. Her mother said "honey, he just wanted to see your underwear."

The next day the same boy was standing by the flagpole and said "I will give you 20 dollars to climb the flagpole." Again she agrees and climbs. She goes home and tells her mother "mom the boy paid me to climb the flagpole again, but I outsmarted him this time. I didn't wear any underwear."

Sometimes your best intentions are thwarted because of a lack of understanding.

The Follower

There was a time in the 1940's when Vyacheslav Molotov was Soviet foreign minister. He was a shrewd man and a hard bargainer but worked for Joseph Stalin, who was The Boss. He was once overheard talking to Stalin by Trans-Atlantic telephone during the course of some very intricate negotiations with the West. He said, "Yes, Comrade Stalin," in quiet tones, then again, "Yes, Comrade Stalin, and then, after a considerable wait, "Certainly, Comrade Stalin. Suddenly he was galvanized into emotion. "No, Comrade Stalin," he barked, "No. That's, no. Definitely, no. A thousand times, no!"

After a while, he quieted and it was "Yes, Comrade Stalin," again. The reporter who overheard this was probably never so excited in his life. Clearly, Molotov was daring to oppose the dictator on at least one point, and it would surely be important to the West to know what that point might be.

The reporter approached Molotov and said as calmly as possible, "Secretary Molotov, I could not help but hear you say at one point, 'No, Comrade Stalin.'"

Molotov turned his cold eyes on the reporter and said, "What of it?" "May I ask," said the reporter, cautiously, "What the subject under discussion was at that time?"

"You may," said Molotov. "Comrade Stalin asked me if there was anything which he had said with which I disagreed."

Wise leaders know that any disagreement should not be discussed with outside parties.

The Haircut

A young boy had just gotten his driving permit. He asked his father, who was a minister, if they could discuss the use of the car. His father took him to his study and said to him, "I'll make a deal with you. You bring your grades up, study your Bible a little and get your hair cut and we'll talk about it." The son agreed.

After about a month the boy came back and again asked his father if they could discuss use of the car. They again went to the father's study where his father said, "Son, I've been real proud of you. You have brought your grades up, you've studied your Bible diligently, but you didn't get your hair cut!"

The young man waited a moment and replied, "You know Dad, I've been thinking about that. You know, Samson had long hair, Moses had long hair, Noah had long hair, and even Jesus had long hair...." To which his father replied, "Yes, and they walked every where they went!"

You may think you have proper justification for not holding up your end of the bargain but there is usually another view you haven't thought of.

Churchill and Twain

Winston Churchill and Mark Twain met for the first time in 1900, when Churchill was just coming into prominence as a young statesman. The meeting took place at a dinner in London. During the dinner, they decided to step outside for a smoke.

An observer, Sir William Harcourt, speculated that since both men tended to dominate conversations, the one who got the floor first would keep it. He told others at his table that since Twain was older and more experienced, Churchill's voice would get the first rest it had had in a long time.

When the two return, Harcourt asked the young Churchill if he had enjoyed talking to Twain. Churchill replied with an enthusiastic "Yes." Harcourt then asked Twain if he had a good chat with Churchill. Twain paused, then said, "I had a good smoke."

You don't have to reveal all the information you have to put an to speculation.

Very Presidential

Calvin Coolidge—A Man of Few Words

At a government function in the nineteen-twenties, a young lady approaching President Coolidge, said gushingly, "Oh, Mr. President, I have made a wager with a friend of mine that I could persuade you to say more than two words to me. Could you?" And Coolidge, without expression, said, "You lose."

Calvin Coolidge, famous for his silence, had been to church. When he returned, he said nothing about the service. His wife prompted him. "What was the sermon about?" she asked. "Sin," Coolidge answered. "Well, what did the preacher say about sin?" she asked impatiently. "He was against it."

Bill Clinton On Running a Country

President Clinton once said running a country is a lot like running a cemetery—you've got a lot of people under you and nobody's listening.

Jack Kennedy—Buying An Election

In March 15, 1958 a young politician in his 40's by the name of Jack Kennedy went to the spotlight. Kennedy's opening line became part of his legend. Previously, his father John had been lampooned in the press as trying to use his family's money and influence to buy the election. Reaching into his pocket Jack, pulled out a telegram he said he had just received from his dad. It said, "Dear Jack, Don't buy a single vote more than is necessary. I'll be damned if I'm going to pay for a landslide."

Test Your Judging Skills

It is time to elect the world leader, and your vote counts. Here are the facts about the three leading candidates:

Candidate A
Associates with crooked politicians, and consults with astrologers. He's had two mistresses. He also chain smokes and drinks quite a few martinis a day.

Candidate B
He was kicked out of office twice, sleeps until noon, used opium in college and drinks a great deal of whisky every evening.

Candidate C
He is a decorated war hero. He's a vegetarian, doesn't smoke, drinks an occasional beer and hasn't had any extramarital affairs.

Which of these candidates would be your choice? Decide before finding out who they are.
Candidate A is Franklin D. Roosevelt
Candidate B is Winston Churchill
Candidate C is Adolph Hitler

A couple of lessons gleaned for leaders are, things are not always what they appear and a few vices might not be such a bad thing!

What Every Team Needs

Every athletic team should have a man who plays every position, never makes an error and knows just what the opposition is planning. But, so far, there's been no way to get him to put down his popcorn and drink to come down out of the stands!

Know Who To Follow

Two men are sitting drinking at a bar at the top of the Empire State Building when the first man turns to the other and says, "You know, last week I discovered that if you jump from the top of this building, by the time you fall to the 10th floor, the winds around the building are so intense that they carry you around the building and back into the window." The bartender just shakes his head in disapproval while wiping the bar.

The second guy says, "What, are you a nut? There is no way that could happen." "No, it's true," said the first man, "let me prove it to you." He gets up from the bar, jumps over the balcony, and plummets to the street below. When he passes the 10th floor, the high wind whips him around the building and back into the 10th floor window and he takes the elevator back up to the bar. He met the second man, who looked quite astonished. "You know, I saw that with my own eyes, but that must have been a one time fluke."

"No, I'll prove it again," says the first man as he jumps. Again just as he is hurling toward the street, the 10th floor wind gently carries him around the building and into the window. Once upstairs he urges his fellow drinker to try it.

"Well, what the hell," the second guy says, "it works, I'll try it!" He jumps over the balcony plunges downward, passes the 11th, 10th, 9th, 8th floors ...and hits the sidewalk with a *Splat.* Back upstairs the bartender turns to the other drinker, saying "You know, Superman, sometimes you can be a real asshole."

Just because one person can do something doesn't mean that everyone can.

The Democrat

While delivering a campaign speech one day a Republican candidate was interrupted by a heckler: "I'm a Democrat!" the man shouted.

"May I ask the gentleman," the candidate replied, quieting the crowd, "why he is a Democrat?"

"My grandfather was a Democrat, my father was a Democrat and I am a Democrat."

"My friend," the candidate interjected, moving in for the kill, "suppose your grandfather had been a jackass and your father was a jackass. What would you then be?"

"A Republican!"

Baiting someone may not always led to the response you are hoping for.

Fishing Equipment

A couple went on vacation to a fishing resort. The husband liked to fish at the crack of dawn and his wife preferred to read. One morning the husband returned after several hours of fishing and decided to take a nap. The wife, to escape her snoring husband, decided to take the boat out. Since she was not familiar with the lake, she rowed out to the middle, anchored the boat, and started reading her book.

Along came a sheriff in his boat. He pulled up alongside and said, "Good morning, ma'am. What are you doing here?"

"Reading a book," she replied, thinking, "Is this guy blind or what?"

"You're in a restricted fishing area," he informed her. "But, Officer, I'm not fishing. You can see that, surely."

"But you have all the equipment, ma'am. I'll have to write you up."

"If you do that, I will charge you with rape," returned the irate woman.

"But I haven't even touched you," the sheriff objected.

"That's true; but you have all the equipment."

Moral? Never argue with anyone who reads!

The Truth Hurts

When Harry was a young boy in Louisiana, he was always getting into trouble. One morning while waiting for the school bus, he pushed the outhouse into the bayou and went off for school as if nothing had happened.

When he returned, his father was waiting for him. He said, "Son, did you push the outhouse into the bayou?" "Yes, father," said Harry, "like George Washington, I cannot tell a lie."

Harry's father took off his belt and said, "All right, son, bend over. I'm going to have to whip you." Harry tried to explain that Mr. Washington didn't spank George when he admitted chopping down the cherry tree. "Yes, son," said Harry's father, "but George's father wasn't in the tree."

Telling the truth has its own set of consequences.

The Pro Bowl With Bill Belichick

Tony Gonzalez played in 14 Pro Bowls—he loved playing when it was in Hawaii. Things were always so relaxing there, so fun. One year, Bill Belichick was his coach, and Gonzalez was curious what made this guy so good. Great players are as bedazzled by Bill Belichick's magic as anyone else. They have all played for good coaches. They have heard all the inspirational stories, all been screamed at for not doing something right, all been shown something on tape that perfectly foreshadowed what they would see in the game. What's so different about this guy?

On the opening kickoff, Gonzalez was out on special teams—there are no backup players at the Pro Bowl, so the stars have to do some menial things—and he went through the motions and didn't block anybody. Gonzalez jogged happily to the sidelines. "Why don't you fucking block somebody Gonzalez," Belichick grumbled as Gonzalez jogged by.

What? Did he just say that? Gonzalez turned and Belichick was just glaring at him, "like I was a piece of shit." Gonzalez felt himself fuming. This was how the great Bill Belichick treated people? They were at the Pro Bowl, for crying out loud. This was Hawaii, for crying out loud. It was a beautiful day, blue sky, blue water, this was supposed to be a reward, a way to honor Gonzalez for working absurdly hard and having another extraordinary season. And this was what he gets? To have the game's most famous coach swear at him for not blocking on special teams in an exhibition game?

Oh, yes, he was mad—who did this guy think he was? Gonzalez played football the right way. He didn't deserve this. He stewed on the sideline, furious. And then it was time to go back on the field for another kickoff, another special teams moment, and the ball was kicked. Gonzalez locked in on a guy running down the field. "Why don't you fucking block somebody?" He heard it again. OK coach, fine, check out this block. And Gonzalez absolutely mashed the defender, took him completely out of the play.

Then Gonzalez walked over to the sideline, and you better believe he walked right by Belichick, he wanted to see the grimace wiped right off the man's face. But Belichick showed no signs of even noticing him. He was looking out on the field, seemingly oblivious to Gonzalez's presence. So Gonzalez kept walking. And as he was a few steps away, he heard Bill Belichick say "Nice block, Gonzalez."

He looked back, and there was no hint of a smile on Belichick's face. Bill Belichick just kept looking at the field, and in that moment Tony Gonzalez understood.

The man had coached him into blocking on special teams even in the Pro Bowl.

Mama K's advice

In the summer of 1992, when he was still in the glow of Duke winning back-to-back national championships, Mike Krzyzewski was sitting on his porch in North Carolina with his wife, his three daughters and his mom.

"Mike, why you?" his mother asked. "What do you mean, Mom?" he replied.

"Why were you the one to win two national championships?" she said, in a way that only a mother could ask a man who was on his way to becoming the greatest coach in the history of men's college basketball.

"Mom, 'Why me' is you." Coach K explained. "I never thought I could lose because of you."

The best advice he ever got, he told his mother, was something she had said to him before he started high school.

"You said to make sure that I only let good people on my bus and if I ever get on someone else's bus, make sure to take it to great places."

The Replay

Jack, a handsome man, walked into a sports bar around 9:58 pm. He sat down next to drunk at the bar and stared up at the TV. The 10:00 news came on. The news crew was covering a story of a man on a ledge of a large building preparing to jump. The drunk looked at Jack and said, "Do you think he'll jump?" Jack says, "You know what, I bet he will." The drunk guy replied, "Well, I bet he won't."" Jack placed 30 dollars on the bar and said, "You're on!"

Just as the drunk placed his money on the bar, the guy did a swan dive off of the building, falling to his death. The drunk was very upset and handed his 30 dollars to Jack, saying, "Fair's fair. Here's your money."

Jack replied, "I can't take your money, I saw this earlier on the 5 o'clock news and knew he would jump."

The drunk guy replies, "I saw it too; but I didn't think he'd do it again."

Jack took the money.

Even the most obvious things can be viewed differently.

The Confused Motorist

A motorist was about two hours from San Diego when he was flagged down by a man whose truck had broken down. The man walked up to the car and asked, "Are you going to San Diego?"

"Sure," answered the motorist "do you need a lift?"

"Not for me. I'll be spending the next three hours fixing my truck. My problem is I've got two chimpanzees in the back which have to be taken to the San Diego Zoo. They're a bit stressed already so I don't want to keep them on the road all day. Could you possibly take them to the zoo for me? I'll give you 100 dollars for your trouble."

"I'd be happy to," said the motorist. So the two chimpanzees were ushered into the back seat of the car and carefully strapped into their seat belts. Off they went.

Five hours later, the truck driver was driving through the heart of San Diego when suddenly he was horrified! There was the motorist walking down the street and holding hands with the two chimps, much to the amusement of a big crowd.

With a screech of brakes he pulled off the road and ran over to the motorist. "What in the world are you doing here?" he demanded. "I gave you 100 dollars to take these chimpanzees to the zoo."

"Yes, I know you did," said the motorist, "but we had money left over— so now we're going to Sea World."

Be very clear about what you want when giving instructions or asking for favors.

The Farmer's Daughter

On a long walk in the woods, Jack found himself out late and decided to look for a place to rest the night. He finally found a hut in the middle of the woods and knocked on the door. An old man answered, and he agreed to give Jack a bed for the night on one condition—the man's daughter would be in the other bed, and Jack was not to touch her or disturb her in any way.

Jack agreed, but changed his mind when he saw how beautiful the sleeping girl was. Jack snuck into her room and cuddled with her, while she didn't respond to his caresses, she didn't push him away either.

The next morning, Jack awoke alone, but he figured the girl had gone to do her chores and he eagerly awaited her return. Instead the old man walked in, wiping the tears from his eyes.

"What's wrong?" asked Jack. "Oh, I've just come back from the cemetery. We had my daughter's funeral this morning. But thank you so much for sitting up with her body last night.

Moral—When told not to do something, either ask for the reason why or simply don't do it!

The Priest and Nun in Winter

A priest and a nun were lost in a snowstorm. After a while, they came upon a small cabin. Being exhausted, they prepared to go to sleep. There was a stack of blankets in the corner and a sleeping bag on the floor but only one bed. Being a gentleman, the priest said, "Sister, you sleep on the bed. I'll sleep on the floor in the sleeping bag."

Just as he got zipped up in the bag and was beginning to fall asleep, the nun said, "Father, I'm cold." He unzipped the sleeping bag, got up, got a blanket and put it on her.

Once again, he got into the sleeping bag, zipped it up and started to drift off to sleep when the nun once again said, "Father, I'm still very cold." He unzipped the bag, got up again, put another blanket on her and got into his sleeping bag once again.

Just as his eyes closed, she said, "Father, I'm sooooo cold." This time, he remained there and said, "Sister, I have an idea. We're out here in the wilderness where no one will ever know what happened. Let's pretend we're married." The nun purred, "That sounds really good to me!"

To which the priest yelled back, "Get up and get your own damn blanket!"

You may think you are on the same page with someone when in fact you are miles apart.

Small Fish

There lived a bear by a riverside in a jungle. One day, he felt hungry. The bear went to the river to catch some fish. Standing by the side of the river, he stared into the water. Soon enough, he saw a fish. He pounced on the fish, and caught it.

But then, the bear thought, "This is too small a fish to fill my stomach. I must catch a bigger fish." So, he let off the small fish. He waited for some time, till he caught another fish. This time too the fish was small.

He thought that the small fish would not fill his belly. So he again let the fish go off. This way he caught many small fish, but let all of them go off, still thinking that the small fish would not fill his belly. By sunset, the bear had not caught any big fish.

He began to feel sorry for having let off so many fish. He realized that all those small fish, together would have filled up his belly, but now it was too late. He had to remain hungry that day.

Always remember a small fish in hand is worth a big fish in the water.

The Nudist's Grandmother

A man moves into a nudist colony. He receives a letter from his mother asking him to send her a current picture. But being too embarrassed to let her know that he lives in a nudist colony, he cuts a photo in half and sends her the top part.

Later, he receives another letter asking him to send a picture to his grandmother. The man cuts another picture in half, but accidentally sends her the bottom half. He is really worried when he realizes that he sent the wrong part, but then remembers how bad his grandmother's eyesight is and hopes she won't notice.

A few weeks later he receives a letter from his grandmother. It says, "Thank you for the picture. Change your hair style—it makes your nose look long!"

People can look at the same thing and see things very differently.

The Pickle Slicer

Bill worked in a pickle factory. He had been employed there for a number of years when he came home one day to confess to his wife that he had a terrible compulsion. He had this urge to stick his penis into the pickle slicer. His wife suggested that he should see a sex therapist to talk about it, but Bill indicated that he'd be too embarrassed. He vowed to overcome the compulsion on his own.

One day, a few weeks later, Bill came home absolutely ashen. His wife could see at once that something was seriously wrong. "What's wrong, Bill?" she asked. "Do you remember that I told you how I had this tremendous urge to put my penis into the pickle slicer?"

"Oh my God Bill, you didn't."

"Yes, I did."

"My God, Bill, what happened are you okay?"

"I got fired."

"No, Bill. I mean, what happened with the pickle slicer?"

"Oh...she got fired too."

Never assume you know all the facts even when someone is confiding in you.

Poked in Church

One day Mrs. Jones went to have a talk with the minister at her local church. "Reverend," she said, "I have a problem. My husband keeps falling asleep during your sermons. It's very embarrassing. What should I do?"

"I have an idea," said the minister. "Take this hatpin with you. I will be able to tell when Mr. Jones is sleeping, and I will nod to you at specific times. When I nod, you give him a good poke in the leg."

In church the following Sunday, Mr. Jones dozed off. Noticing this, the preacher put his plan to work. "And who made the ultimate sacrifice for you?" he said, nodding to Mrs. Jones.

"Jesus!" Mr. Jones cried as his wife jabbed him in the leg with the hatpin.

"Yes, you are right, my son," said the minister.

Soon, Mr. Jones nodded off again. Again, the minister noticed. "Who is your redeemer?" he asked the congregation, motioning towards Mrs. Jones.

"God!" Mr. Jones cried out as he was stuck again with the hatpin.

"Right again," said the minister, smiling.

Before long, Mr. Jones again dozed off. However, this time the minister did not notice. As he picked up the tempo of his sermon, he made a few motions that Mrs. Jones mistook as signals to bayonet her husband with the hatpin again.

The minister asked, "And what did Eve say to Adam after she bore him another son?"

Mrs. Jones poked her husband, who yelled, "You stick that damned thing in me one more time and I'll break it off and shove it up your ass!"

Not all answers are relevant to the question asked.

The Painting Nuns

Two nuns are ordered to paint a room that was under construction in the convent, and the last instruction of the Mother Superior is that they must not get even a drop of paint on their habits.

After conferring about this for a while, the two nuns decide to lock the door of the room, strip off their habits, and paint in the nude.

In the middle of the project, there comes a knock at the door. "Who is it?" calls out one of the nuns.

"Blind man," replies a male voice from the other side of the door. The two nuns look at each other, shrug, and deciding that no harm can come from letting a blind man into the room, they open the door.

"Nice breasts, sister," says the man, "Where do you want these blinds?"

Always ask for clarity because words sometimes have double meanings.

My Name Is...

There once was an overprotective farmer whose wife had died and left him with three beautiful teenage daughters. Every weekend, when they went out on dates, the farmer would stand at the door with his shotgun, making it clear to their dates he wanted no trouble from them.

Another Saturday night came around. About 7 p.m., there was a knock on the door. He answered and the young man said, "Hi, my name's Joe. I'm taking your daughter to the show. Don't worry sir, we will take it slow. Is she ready to go?" The farmer thought he was a clever boy and wished them a good time.

A few minutes later, another knock was heard. A second boy appeared and said, "Hi, I'm Eddie. I'm taking your daughter for spaghetti. We plan to met with her friend named Betty. I hope she's ready." He thought that he must know Joe, but bade them off as well with his best wishes.

A few minutes after that, a third knock was heard. "Hi, I'm Chuck..." The farmer shot him.

There are times when things are taken out on you simply because of those that have come before you.

Wise Old Couple

An elderly couple went into a doctor. They told the doctor, "We're having some trouble with our sex life. Could you watch and offer some suggestions?"

The doctor replied, "I'm not a sex therapist. You should find someone else."

The couple said, "No, no, we trust you."

After watching them have sex, the doctor said, "You don't seem to be having any troubles. I wish my sex life was as good. I can't give you any suggestions."

This was repeated the next week and also the third week. After they had finished on the third week, the doctor said, "You aren't having any trouble at all. Is this your idea of kinky sex?"

The man replied, "No, actually the problem is if we have sex at my house, my wife will catch us. If we have sex at her house, her husband will catch us. The motel charges us 50 dollars, but you only charge 35, and medicare pays half of that."

As much as leaders want to help, it's always a good idea to get the real reason why someone comes to you with their problems.

Exposing Gardening Secrets

Once there was a woman who loved to work in her vegetable garden, but no matter what she did, she couldn't get her tomatoes to ripen. Admiring her wise old neighbor's garden, which had beautiful, bright red tomatoes, she went one day and inquired about his secret. "It's really quite simple," the man explained, "Twice each day, in the morning and in the evening, I get naked and expose myself in front of the tomatoes and they turn red with embarrassment."

Desperate for the perfect garden, she tried his advice and proceeded to expose herself to her tomato plants, twice daily. Two weeks passed and her neighbor stopped by to check on her progress. "So," he asked, "Any luck with your tomatoes?"

"No," she replied excitedly, "but you should see the size of the cucumbers!"

Taking the advice of a wise person can lead to unexpected benefits.

You Have Sinned

Jerry, Kenny, and Larry found themselves in Hell. They were a little confused at their present situation and were startled to see a door in the wall open. Behind the door was perhaps the ugliest woman they had ever seen. She was dirty, and they could smell her even over the Brimstone.

The voice of the Devil boomed out, "Jerry, you have sinned! You are condemned to spend the rest of eternity in bed with this woman!" And Jerry was whisked through the door by a group of lesser demons to his eternal torment.

This understandably shook up the other two, and so they both jumped when a second door opened, and they saw an even more disgusting example of womanhood gone wrong. She was huge, covered in thick black hair, and flies circled her. The voice of the Devil was heard again, louder than before, "Kenny, you have sinned! You are condemned to spend the rest of eternity in bed with this woman!" And Kenny, like Jerry, was whisked off, screaming and scratching, to his doom.

Larry, now alone, felt understandably anxious, and feared the worst when the third door opened. And as the door inched open, he strained to see the figure of Cindy, the sexiest woman he has ever seen. Delighted, Larry jumped up, taking in the sight of this beautiful woman barely dressed in a skimpy bikini. Then he heard the voice of the Devil booming: "Cindy, you have sinned..."

While something may be good for it; others may see it as a living hell.

Mama Doesn't Understand

Maria just got married, and being a traditional Italian, she was still a virgin. So, on her wedding night, staying at her mother's house, she was nervous. But her mother reassured her. "Don't worry, Maria. Tony is a good man. Go upstairs, and he'll take care of you." So up she went. When she got upstairs, Tony took off his shirt and exposed his hairy chest.

Maria ran downstairs to her mother and says, "Mama, mama, Tony's got a big hairy chest." "Don't worry, Maria", says the mother, "All good men have hairy chests. Go upstairs. He'll take good care of you."

So, up she went again. When she got up in the bedroom, Tony took off his pants exposing his hairy legs. Again Maria ran downstairs to her mother. "Mama, Mama, Tony took off his pants, and he's got hairy legs, too!" "Don't worry. All good men have hairy legs. Tony is a good man. Go upstairs, and he'll take good care of you."

So, up she went again. When she got up there, Tony took off his socks, and part of his left foot was missing. When Maria saw this, she ran downstairs. "Mama, Mama, Tony's got a foot and a half!"

"Stay here and stir the pasta", says the mother, "this is a job for Mama!"

Jumping to conclusions is never a good idea.

The Genie

A man and his wife were playing golf. The man tees off and his ball veers way off to the right, breaking the window of a house. The wife says you must go and apologize and pay for the window.

Both the man and his wife walk up to the house, ring the door but no one answers. He opens the door and inside, next to the window he sees a broken vase with his golf ball laying on the floor. Suddenly a man comes out of a nearby room, the golfer starts to apologize for breaking his window and the vase.

The man inside the house says, "No, don't apologize, I am a genie and have been stuck in that vase for 10,000 years, you have rescued me and I owe you deeply. For helping me I will grant three wishes. I will give you one, your lovely wife one and I would like to keep one for myself."

He asks the man what he wishes for. The man thought awhile and said, "I wish for a million dollars." The genie waves his hand and said, "A million dollars, it's yours, it has been deposited into your bank account."

He asks the wife what is her wish. She says, "I wish for condominium in Hawaii." The genie waves his hand and says, "A condominium in Hawaii, it's yours." The genie continues, "Now it is my turn." He thinks for awhile and says, "You know its been 10,000 years since I have had a woman, could I make love to your wife?"

The man thinks for a while and says, "Honey, he gave us a million dollars and a condominium in Hawaii, the least you could do is make love to him." She agrees and they both go to the back bedroom.

After making passionate love, the woman says, "I can't believe that my husband agreed to this."

The genie says, "And I can't believe that your husband still believes in genies."

There are a lot of people who make promises and pretend to be something they are not in order to get what they want

A Lesson In Politics

A little boy goes to his dad and asks, "What is politics?" Dad says, "Well son, let me try to explain it this way: I'm the breadwinner of the family, so let's call me Capitalism. Your Mom, she's the administrator of the money, so we'll call her the Government. We're here to take care of your needs, so we'll call you the People. The nanny, we'll consider her the Working Class. And your baby brother, we'll call him the Future. Now, think about that and see if that makes sense."

So the little boy goes off to bed thinking about what Dad has said. Later that night, he hears his baby brother crying, so he gets up to check on him. He finds that the baby has severely soiled his diaper. So the little boy goes to his parents' room and finds his mother sound asleep. Not wanting to wake her, he goes to the nanny's room. Finding the door locked, he peeks in the keyhole and sees his father in bed with the nanny. He gives up and goes back to bed.

The next morning, the little boy says to his father, "Dad, I think I understand the concept of politics now."

The father says, "Good, son, tell me in your own words what you think politics is all about."

The little boy replies, "Well, while Capitalism is screwing the Working Class, the Government is sound asleep, the People are being ignored and the Future is in Deep Shit."

Explanations are better interpreted through observations so make sure your actions align with what lessons you want taught.

Bear Bryant:
A Lesson About Dealing With People

At a touchdown club meeting many years before his death, Coach Paul "Bear" Bryant told the following story, which was typical of the way he operated.

I had just been named the new head coach at Alabama and was off in my old car down in South Alabama recruiting a prospect who was supposed to have been a pretty good player and I was havin' trouble finding the place.

Getting hungry I spied an old cinder block building with a small sign out front that simply said "Restaurant." I pull up, go in and every head in the place turns to stare at me. Seems I'm the only white 'fella' in the place. But the food smelled good so I skip a table and go up to a cement bar and sit.

A big ole man in a tee shirt and cap comes over and says, "What do you need?" I told him I needed lunch and what did they have today? He says, "You probably won't like it here, today we're having chitlins, collared greens and black eyed peas with cornbread. I'll bet you don't even know what chitlins are, do you?" I looked him square in the eye and said, "I'm from Arkansas, I've probably eaten a mile of them. Sounds like I'm in the right place." They all smiled as he left to serve me up a big plate.

When he comes back he says, "You ain't from around then?" And I explain I'm the new football coach up in Tuscaloosa at the University and I'm here to find whatever that boy's name was and he says, "Yeah I've heard of him, he's supposed to be pretty good." And he gives me directions to the school so I can meet him and his coach.

As I'm paying up to leave, I remember my manners and leave a tip, not too big to be flashy, but a good one and he told me lunch was on him, but I told him for a lunch that good, I felt I should pay. The big man asked me if I had a photograph or something he could hang up to show I'd been there. I was so new that I didn't have any yet. It really wasn't that big a thing back then to be asked for, but I took a napkin and wrote his name and address on it and told him I'd get him one.

I met the kid I was 'lookin' for later that afternoon and I don't remember his name, but do remember I didn't think much of him when I met him. I had wasted a day, or so I thought. When I got back to Tuscaloosa late that night, I took that napkin from my shirt pocket and put it under my keys so I wouldn't forget it. Heck, back then I was excited that anybody would want a picture of me. And the next day we found a picture and I

(Continued on page 66)

(Continued from page 65)

wrote on it, Thanks for the best lunch I've ever had, Paul Bear Bryant.

Now let's go a whole 'buncha' years down the road. Now we have black players at Alabama and I'm back down in that part of the country scouting an offensive lineman we sure needed. Y'all remember, and I forget the name, but it's not important to the story, well anyway, he's got two friends going to Auburn and he tells me he's got his heart set on Auburn too, so I leave empty handed and go on to see some others while I'm down there.

Two days later, I'm in my office in Tuscaloosa and the phone rings and it's this kid who just turned me down, and he says, "Coach, do you still want me at Alabama ?" And I said, "Yes I sure do." And he says, o.k. he'll come. And I say, "Well son, what changed your mind?" And he said, "When my grandpa found out that I had a chance to play for you and said no, he pitched a fit and told me I wasn't going nowhere but Alabama and wasn't playing for nobody but you. He thinks a lot of you and has ever since y'all met."

Well, I didn't know his granddad from Adam's housecat so I asked him who his granddaddy was and he said, "You probably don't remember him, but you ate in his restaurant your first year at Alabama and you sent him a picture that he's had hung in that place ever since. That picture's his pride and joy and he still tells everybody about the day that Bear Bryant came in and had chitlins with him. My grandpa said that when you left there, he never expected you to remember him or to send him that picture, but you kept your word to him and to Grandpa, that's everything. He said you could teach me more than football and I had to play for a man like you, so I guess I'm going to."

I was floored. But I learned that the lessons my mama taught me were always right. It don't cost nuthin' to be nice. It don't cost 'nuthin' to do the right thing most of the time, and it costs a lot to lose your good name by breakin' your word to someone. When I went back to sign that boy, I looked up his Grandpa and he's still running that place, but it looks a lot better now; and he didn't have chitlins that day, but he had some ribs that 'woulda' made Dreamland proud and I made sure I posed for a lot of pictures; and don't think I didn't leave some new ones for him, too, along with a signed football.

I made it clear to all my assistants to keep this story and these lessons in mind when they're out on the road. And if you remember anything else from me, remember this – It really doesn't cost anything to be nice, and the rewards can be unimaginable.

Coach Bryant was in the presence of these few gentlemen for only minutes, and he defined himself for life, to these gentlemen, as a nice man.

Coach K Hangs Up

Have you ever wondered what makes a good player great? What's the edge they hold over another player with the same size and athletic ability? Or sometimes, there are players who have neither size nor athletic ability, but through sheer will, they walk into any arena and conquer. Coach K tells the story of how he willed Shane Battier to be a star by calling him every day and asking him specific thought-provoking questions.

One summer morning in 1999, he called Shane Battier, a rising junior at the time, and asked him if he had looked in the mirror and seen next year's conference player of the year. When Battier fumbled his words, Coach hung up.

The next day he called the 6'8" forward and asked him if he had pictured himself scoring 30 points in any game the following season. Battier was clearly not ready for that question either, so he encountered another dead phone. It was after that 1998-1999 season when Duke saw four productive players leave from a team that lost in the 1999 national championship to UConn, giving Jim Calhoun his first title. Trajan Langdon graduated. Elton Brand, a sophomore at the time, decided to go pro and was the first overall draft pick to the Michael Jordan-less Chicago Bulls. William Avery, a sophomore, got drafted 14th by the Minnesota Timberwolves. Freshman Corey Maggette got drafted just before Avery by the now-defunct Seattle Supersonics.

If when it rains it pours, it certainly was a storm for Duke that summer. Coach K had never had a player leave Duke before graduating up to that time, but then not one, but three players left early. Had that team played another year together, the Blue Devils would have at least made the Final Four again. However that was not to be, so Coach K had to form another plan. Make Shane Battier, a role player on that 1998-1999 team, a star. This was made more difficult, because the player had never imagined himself as a star. After the second call, Battier called his coach back, asking him not to hang up on him again. Coach K replied, "I won't hang up on you if you won't hang up on you."

How many times have we seen players who are so blessed with talent and ability but just don't believe in themselves?

Wojo—How I Got Recruited to Duke

"I remember seeing Coach Krzyzewski at my games the summer before my high school senior year. When he walks into a gym, he carries such a big presence. It's a special thing. ... I kind of fell into being a high-major player the summer before my senior year. I thought I'd end up at the Ivys. But I went to the 5-Star Camp and ended up getting MVP. ... There was one extra spot, and it was a spot on a team with nine Russians. None of them spoke English. We had a great week. I went from being recruited by Penn and Princeton to Duke, North Carolina, Wake Forest. I wasn't very tall, not jet-quick or a great shooter. I was a leader. Coach K was asking assistant coach, Mike Brey: 'Is this kid good enough?' And Coach K always tells this story, that Coach Brey told him, 'If he can lead nine Russians, he can lead anyone.'

—Steve Wojciechowski

A Pigeon Poops on Wooden

This story comes from a ceremony for the inaugural members of the National Collegiate Basketball Hall of Fame in 2006 in Kansas City, Mo., where John Wooden was honored along with Dean Smith, Bill Russell, Oscar Robertson and posthumously James Naismith.

At age 96, Wooden was back at the site of his first NCAA championship in 1964, prompting him to recall a message he had received "from above" right after the beginning of his 10-championship run at UCLA. "We won on a Saturday night," Wooden said. "I planned on going out Easter Sunday, my wife and I. Sunday morning, we were outside the Muehlebach Hotel, waiting to get a cab to take us to the church. And a pigeon pooped right on the top of my head.

And I felt, 'Well, we just won the national championship, the team did, don't let it go to your head.' And I think the Good Lord was letting me know, 'Don't get carried away.' I'll always remember that."

The Perfect Preacher

A preacher was walking down the street when he came upon a group of a few boys about 10 years old, surrounding a dog. Concerned that the boys were hurting the animal, he went over and asked them what they were doing. One of the boys replied, "This dog is an old neighborhood stray. Sometimes, we take turns taking him home with us, but it's been awhile since we've seen the dog so we're having a contest—whichever one of us tells the biggest lie can take him home today."

The preacher was shocked and exclaimed, "You boys shouldn't be having a contest telling lies!" He then launched into a sermon against lying—"Don't you boys know it's a sin to lie?" He ended with "Why when I was your age, I never told a lie." There was complete silence. As the preacher smiled with satisfaction thinking he'd gotten through to them, the smallest boy gave a deep sigh. "All right, give him the dog."

Preaching how perfect you are may send you home with more than you bargained for.

New Year's Lecture

On New Year's Eve, Daniel was in no shape to drive, so he sensibly left his vehicle in the parking lot and walked home. As he was wobbling along, he was stopped by a policeman.

"What are you doing out here at four o'clock in the morning?" asked the police officer.

"I'm on my way to a lecture," answered Daniel.

"And who on earth, in their right mind, is going to give a lecture at this time on New Year's Eve?" enquired the officer sarcastically.

"My wife," slurred Daniel grimly.

More than one question is often required to get the real story.

The Accident

A woman and a man get into a car accident. Neither of them were hurt but both cars could not be driven. At first glance it is hard to determine who is at fault. After they crawl out of their cars, the woman says, "Wow! So you're a handsome man, that's interesting. And I think I am a good looking woman, don't you think? The good thing is we are both not hurt. This must be a sign from God that we should meet and become friends if you know what I mean."

"Yes! I agree with you completely—you are beautiful and yes this must be a sign from God," said the man.

The woman continued, "And look at this—here's another miracle. My car is completely demolished but this bottle of wine didn't break. Surely God wants us to drink this wine and celebrate our good fortune."

So she hands the bottle to the man. The man nods his head in agreement, smiles knowingly, opens it and takes several huge swigs from the bottle. He then hands it back to the woman.

The woman takes the bottle, immediately puts the cap back on, and hands it back to the man.

The man takes the bottle and asks, "Aren't you having any?" The woman replies, "No. I think I will just wait for the police."

Be very clear of the motives of someone before taking action—especially those you have no prior relationship with.

The Maid Ask For A Raise

Claire, the maid of the house, decided to ask for a raise and set up a meeting with the wife and husband for whom she worked. The wife didn't think she deserved a raise and became loud and very boisterous during the conversation. She asked, "Now, Claire, why do you think you deserve a pay increase?"

Claire: "There are three reasons. The first is that I iron better than you."

Wife: "Who said that?"

Claire: "Your husband."

Wife: "Oh."

Claire: "The second reason is that I am a better cook than you."

Wife: "Who said that?"

Claire: "Your husband."

Wife: "Oh." The wife was getting angrier by the minute while the husband just sat by quietly.

Claire: And the third reason is that I am better at sex than you."

Wife: "WHAT! Did my husband say that as well?"

Claire: "No, the gardener did."

During a heated negotiation you never know when information can and will be used against you.

Rex's Old Lady

One day, an old woman was sitting in her rocking chair on her front porch. Beside her slept her mangy, old dog, Rex. Suddenly, a genie appeared, startling the woman. "Old woman," the genie said, "I felt sorry for you sitting here looking old and tired, so I decided to grant you three wishes." The woman thought about it and said, "Well, I've always wanted to be a young, beautiful princess."

Poof! The genie turned her into a young, beautiful princess. The princess thought some more and said, "A princess should live in a castle, so could you do something about this old shack?"

Poof! The old shack was transformed into a huge castle.

Again the princess thought then asked, "Shouldn't a beautiful princess have a handsome prince?" The genie looked around and spotted Rex.

Poof! Rex was transformed into a handsome Prince. "Well, my work here is done," the genie said and he disappeared in a puff of smoke. The princess gazed at Rex the handsome prince and felt her heart beating rapidly for he was the most handsome man she had ever seen. Rex, the handsome prince, strolled up to the beautiful princess and kissed her passionately. She melted in his arms and cried, "Take me Rex! Take me now!"

Rex then whispered in her ear, "Bet you're sorry that you had me neutered now!"

The things you do to someone else always have a chance of affecting you later.

Christmas Shopping

In the week before Christmas Cara, a very pretty young girl sauntered up to the curtain counter trying to decide which of the many types of tinsel she would buy. Finally, she made her choice and asked the spotty young man who was manning the fabric section, "How much is this gold tinsel garland?"

The haughty youth pointed to the Christmas mistletoe above the counter and said, "This week we have a special offer, just one kiss per yard."

"Wow, that's great," said Cara, "I'll take 12 yards." With expectation and anticipation written all over his face, the boy measured out the tinsel, wrapped up the garland, and gave it to Cara.

She then called to an old man who had been browsing through the Christmas trees and said, "My Grandpa will settle the bill."

Be very specific about what you expect in return anytime anyone asks something of you.

Out-Smarting The Professor

Kevin's chemistry professor wanted to teach his class a lesson about the evils of liquor, so he set up an experiment that involved a glass of water, a glass of whiskey, and two worms.

"Now, class. Observe what happens to the two the worms," said the professor putting the first worm in the glass of water. The worm in the water moved about, twisting and seemingly unharmed.

He then dropped the second work in the whiskey glass. It writhed in pain for a moment, then quickly sank to the bottom and died. "Now kids, what lesson can we derive from this experiment?" he asked.

Kevin raised his hand and wisely responded, "If you drink whiskey every day, you won't get worms!"

No matter how much you try, how something is interpreted is up to each individual.

The People Who Get Noticed

A large organization had recently hired several cannibals. After conducting a lengthy new hire orientation the human resource director congratulated the cannibals and said, "You are all part of the team now! You get all of the benefits we have discussed and you can enjoy our company cafe free of charge! But please don't eat any of the other employees." Each of the cannibals promised they wouldn't.

After a few weeks the cannibal's boss seemed very pleased, but also a little worried. She said, "You're all working very hard and I'm satisfied with you. However, one of our secretaries has disappeared. Do any of you know what happened to her?" The cannibals all shook their heads, "No."

After the boss left, the leader of the cannibals was a bit angry and said, "Okay, which one of you dummies ate the secretary?" A hand rose hesitantly in admission. "You fool!" said the leader, "For weeks we've been eating managers and no one noticed anything, but nooo, you had to go and eat someone important!."

Never underestimate the value of your secretary!

The Conversation

Person 1: I'm terrified of Muslims. I don't want sharia law in America.

Person 2: OK. Let's avoid that by separating church and state.

1: Nope. I believe in Jesus and want this country to be more Christian.

2: OK. Here are some refugees who need help.

1: Nope. Not helping refugees while we still have homeless kids and veterans here.

2: OK. Here's a bill to help vets.

1: Nope. I don't want to raise taxes.

2: OK. What about homeless kids? Surely they deserve some help.

1: Nope. Their parents are just lazy and want handouts. They shouldn't have had kids if they can't afford kids.

2: OK. Let's fund Planned Parenthood to help people plan their parenthood.

1: Nope. Some of that money might go for an abortion, and I'm Pro Life.

2: OK. Let's give everyone easier access to health care to improve and extend their lives.

1: Nope. That's socialism. I believe in the Constitution, not dirty, dirty socialism.

2: OK. At least we can agree on that. I especially like the way the Constitution gives everyone freedom of and from religion.

1: Yes! Freedom of religion. Except Muslims. I'm terrified of Muslims...

Too often fear is allowed to overcome any attempt at rational thinking.

The Doctor's Visit

A woman and a baby were in the doctor's examining room waiting for the doctor to come in for the baby's first exam.

Finally the doctor arrived, examined the baby, checked his weight. and being a little concerned, asked if the baby was breast-fed or bottle-fed.

"Breast-fed" she replied.

"Well! We'll have to check you out. Alright then, strip down to your waist," "he doctor ordered.

She undressed and the doctor began his exam.

He pinched her nipples, then pressed, kneaded, and rubbed both breasts for a while in a detailed examination. He frowned, then continued squeezing and pressing for a few more minutes.

Motioning to her to get dressed, he said, "No wonder this baby is underweight. You don't have any milk!"

"I know," she said. "I'm his Grandma, but I'm certainly glad I came."

Make sure you know exactly who your advice is being given to.

The Holy Light

An 80 year old man went for his annual check up and the doctor said, "Friend, for your age you're in the best shape I've seen."

The man replied, "Yep. It comes from clean living. In fact, I know I live a good, clean, spiritual life."

The doctor asked, "What makes you say that?"

The old man replied, "If I didn't live such a good, clean life God wouldn't turn the bathroom light on for me every time I get up in the middle of the night.

The doc became concerned. "You mean when you get up in the night to go to the bathroom, God Himself turns on the light for you?"

"Yep," the old man said, "Whenever I get up to go to the bathroom, God turns the light on for me."

Well, the doctor didn't say anything else, but when the old man's wife came in for her check up, he felt he had to let her know what her husband said. "I just want you to know," the doctor said "Your husband's in fine physical shape but I'm worried about his mental condition. He told me that every night when he gets up to go to the bathroom, God turns the light on for him.

"Aha!" she exclaimed. "He's the one who's been peeing in the refrigerator!"

There is usually a simple explanation to a most confounding situations.

A Helping Wife

"Martha, soon we will be married 50 years, and there's something I have to know. In all of these 50 years, have you ever been unfaithful to me?"

Martha replied, "Well Henry, I have to be honest with you.. Yes, I've been unfaithful to you three times during these 50 years, but always for a good reason.

Henry was obviously surprised by his wife's confession, but said, "I never suspected. Can you tell me what you mean by 'good reasons'?"

Martha said, "The first time was shortly after we were married, and we were about to lose our little house because we couldn't pay the mortgage. Do you remember that one evening I went to see the banker and the next day he notified you that the loan would be extended?"

Henry recalled the visit to the banker and said, "I can forgive you for that, you saved our home, but what about the second time?"

Martha asked, "And do you remember when you were got hurt, but we didn't have the money to pay for the surgery you needed? Well, I went to see your doctor one night and, if you recall, he did the surgery at no charge."

"I do recall that," said Henry. "And you did it to save my life, so of course I can forgive you for that. Now tell me about the third time."

"All right," Martha said. "Do you remember when you ran for president of your golf club, and you needed 73 more votes?"

Henry fainted...

It's a good idea to tell those willing to help what parameters you want them to operate within.

Because The Bible Says So

Dr. Laura, a radio personality who dispenses advice to people said that homosexuality is an abomination according to Leviticus 18:22 and cannot be condoned under any circumstance. The following is a funny and informative open letter written by a listener.

Dear Dr. Laura,

Thank you for doing so much to educate people regarding God's Law. When someone tries to defend the homosexual lifestyle, I simply remind them that Leviticus 18:22 clearly states it to be an abomination. End of debate. I do need some advice from you, however, regarding some of the other specific laws and how to follow them:

When I burn a bull on the altar as a sacrifice, I know it creates a pleasing odor for the Lord - Lev.1:9. The problem is my neighbors. They claim the odor is not pleasing to them. Should I smite them?

I would like to sell my daughter into slavery, as sanctioned in Exodus 21:7. In this day and age, what do you think would be a fair price for her?

I know that I am allowed no contact with a woman while she is in her period of menstrual uncleanliness - Lev.15:19- 24. The problem is, how do I tell? I have tried asking, but most women take offense.

Lev. 25:44 states that I may indeed possess slaves, both male and female, provided they are purchased from neighboring nations. A friend of mine claims that this applies to Mexicans, but not Canadians. Can you clarify? Why can't I own Canadians?

I have a neighbor who insists on working on the Sabbath.. Exodus 35:2 clearly states he should be put to death. Am I morally obligated to kill him myself?

A friend of mine feels that even though eating shellfish is an abomination - Lev. 11:10, it is a lesser abomination than homosexuality. I don't agree. Can you settle this?

Lev. 21:20 states that I may not approach the altar of God if I have a defect in my sight. I have to admit that I wear reading glasses. Does my vision have to be 20-20, or is there some wiggle room here?

(Continued on page 80)

(Continued from page 79)

Most of my male friends get their hair trimmed, including the hair around their temples, even though this is expressly forbidden by Lev. 19:27. How should they die?

I know from Lev. 11:6-8 that touching the skin of a dead pig makes me unclean, but may I still play football if I wear gloves?

My uncle has a farm. He violates Lev. 19:19 by planting two different crops in the same field, as does his wife by wearing garments made of two different kinds of thread—cotton-polyester blend. He also tends to curse and blaspheme a lot. Is it really necessary that we go to all the trouble of getting the whole town together to stone them? - Lev.24:10-16. Couldn't we just burn them to death at a private family affair like we do with people who sleep with their in-laws? —Lev. 20:14

I know you have studied these things extensively, since you are so adamant about homosexuality, so I am confident you can help. Thank you again for reminding us that God's word is eternal and unchanging.

Your devoted fan, Jim

Moose Hunting

Two hunters hired a pilot to fly them to Canada to hunt moose. They bagged four moose.

As they started loading the plane for the return trip home, the pilot tells them the plane can take only two moose.

The two professors objected strongly, stating, "Last year we shot four moose, and the pilot let us put them all on board, and he had the same plane as yours."

Reluctantly, the pilot gave in and all four were loaded. Unfortunately, even at full power, the little plane couldn't handle the load and crashed a few minutes after takeoff. Climbing out of the wreck, one hunter asked the other, "Any idea where we are?"

He replied, "I think we're pretty close to where we crashed last year."

You can't keep making silly uniformed requests and expect different results.

Death Row

Three people are all on death row awaiting execution by electric chair. The first person is strapped to the chair and is asked, "Do you have anything you want to say before we throw the switch?" And he says, "Yes sir, I just want to say I'm an innocent man."

The warden chuckles a bit to himself then nods to the man at the switch. The switch is thrown and... absolutely nothing happens. The warden is amazed. "Son, the Lord seems to have given you a second chance. Maybe you really ARE innocent. We're gonna let you go free."

The second person is then strapped to the chair. The warden says, "All right, have you got anything to say?" The person says, "Yes sir. I admit that I did kill that dude, but it was all in self defense. I never did it in cold blood."

The warden chuckles and nods to the man at the switch, who throws it and... absolutely nothing happens. "Well, I'll be damned," says the warden, "you must be tellin' the truth too! Let 'em go, boys!" And they unstrapped him and set him free.

Finally, they bring the third person to the chair and strap him in. The warden says, "Now, do YOU have anything to say?" And he says, "Sure! If you switched that red wire with that green wire over there, this thing would work!"

Sometimes it is in your best interest to keep your mouth shut even if you know what the problem is.

The Young King

A young King was ambushed and imprisoned by the monarch of a neighboring kingdom. The monarch could have killed him but was moved by the King's youth and ideals. So, the monarch offered him his freedom, as long as he could answer a very difficult question. He would have a year to figure out the answer and, if after a year, he still had no answer, he would be put to death. The question?... What do women really want? Such a question would perplex even the most knowledgeable man, and to the young king, it seemed an impossible query. But, since it was better than death, he accepted the monarch's proposition to have an answer by year's end.

He returned to his kingdom and began to poll everyone—the princess, the priests, the wise men and even the court jester. He spoke with everyone, but no one could give him a satisfactory answer. Many people advised him to consult the old witch, for only she would have the answer. But the price would be high; as the witch was famous throughout the kingdom for the exorbitant prices she charged.

The last day of the year arrived and the king had no choice but to talk to the witch. She agreed to answer the question, but he would have to agree to her price first. The old witch wanted to marry the most noble of the Knights of the Round Table and the closest friend of the king. The king was horrified. She was hunchbacked and hideous, had only one tooth, smelled like sewage, made obscene noises, etc. He had never encountered such a repugnant creature in all his life. He refused to force his friend to marry her and endure such a terrible burden; but the Knight, learning of the proposal, spoke with the king. He said nothing was too big of a sacrifice compared to the king's life and the preservation of the Round Table. Hence, a wedding was proclaimed and the witch answered the king's question thus: *What a woman really wants, she answered is to be in charge of her own life.*

Everyone in the kingdom instantly knew that the witch had uttered a great truth and that the king's life would be spared. And so it was, the neighboring monarch granted the king his freedom and the Knight and the witch had a wonderful wedding. The honeymoon hour approached and the Knight, steeling himself for was sure to be a horrific experience, entered the bedroom. But, what a sight awaited him. The most beautiful woman he had ever seen lay before him on the bed. The astounded Knight asked what had happened. The super-sexy lady before him replied that since he had been so kind to her when she appeared as a witch, she would henceforth, be her horrible deformed self only half the time and this beautiful maiden the other half. She asked, "Which would you prefer? Beautiful during the day or night?

(Continued on page 83)

(Continued from page 82)

The Knight pondered the predicament. During the day, a beautiful woman to show off to his friends, but at night, in the privacy of his castle, an old witch? Or, would he prefer having a hideous witch during the day, but by night, a beautiful woman for him to enjoy wondrous intimate moments?

Being the noble Knight he was he said that he would allow her to make the choice herself. Upon hearing this, she announced that she would be beautiful all the time because he had respected her enough to let her be in charge of her own life.

What is the moral to this story? If you don't let a woman have her own way—things are going to get ugly.

Quick—Politically Incorrect—Hitters

Can a woman make you a Millionaire? Yes, if you are a Billionaire.

When a woman says "what?" Its not because she didn't hear you. She's just giving you a chance to change what you said.

Behind every angry woman is a man who has absolutely no idea what he did wrong.

I still remember my father-in-law's last words to me... stop shaking the ladder.

I named my dog 5 miles so I can tell people that I walk 5 miles every single day.

Know why hurricanes started out being named after women? Because when they first come they are wild and wet, and when they leave they take your house and car with them.

In An Effort Of Fairness Here Are More Quick Politically Incorrect Hitters

Husband: "I don't know why you wear a bra; you've got nothing to put in it."
Wife: "You wear pants don't you?"

A husband decided to wash his sweatshirt. Seconds after he stepped into the laundry room, he shouted to his wife, "What setting do I use on the washing machine?""It depends," she replied. "What does it say on your shirt?" He yelled back, "University of North Carolina"

The perfect breakfast for a woman:
> She's sitting at the table with her gourmet coffee.
> Her son is on the cover of the Wheaties box.
> Her daughter is on the cover of Business Week.
> Her boyfriend is on the cover of Playgirl.
> And her husband is on the back of the milk carton

A woman was helping her computer-illiterate husband set up his computer and at the appropriate point in the process it said he would now need to choose and enter a password. The husband figured he would try for the shock effect so, when the computer asked him to enter his password, he made it plainly obvious to his wife that he was keying in, p-e-n-i-s.   His wife fell off her chair laughing when the computer replied: PASSWORD REJECTED. NOT LONG ENOUGH.

How do you keep your husband from reading your e-mail? Rename the mail folder to "instruction manuals"

The reason men get married is so they don't have to hold their stomachs in any more.

Men are like a fine wine. They all start out like grapes, and it's the woman's job to stomp on them and keep them in the dark until they mature into something they'd want to have dinner with.

Bond, James Bond

James Bond walks into a bar and takes a seat next to a very attractive woman. He gives her a quick glance, then casually looks at his watch for a moment. The woman notices this and asks, "Is your date running late?"

"No," he replies. "Q just gave me this state-of-the-art watch and I was just testing it." The intrigued woman says, "A state-of-the-art watch? What's so special about it?"

Bond explains, "It uses alpha waves to talk to me telepathically." The lady says, "What's it telling you now?"

"Well, it says you're not wearing any panties."

The woman giggles and replies, "Well, it must be broken because I am wearing panties!"

Bond tugs, taps his watch and says, "Damn thing is an hour fast."

A good plan is best executed with precision and patience.

Recommendation For The City

Frank was getting ready to go on a trip to New York for the first time, and was talking to his friend Bill.

Bill: "While you are in New York, there is a bar that you have to go to. When you walk through the front door, you are handed a free drink. Then you can go to the back room and have sex. Come back up to the bar, and you get another free drink. Then you can get laid again. It goes on like this all night."

Frank: "That sounds unbelievable. Have you really been there?"

Bill: "No, but my wife has many times."

Recommendations can come from unexpected places.

Men From Mars...

The year is 2222 and Joey and Caroline land on Mars after accumulating enough frequent flier miles. They meet a Martian couple and are talking about all sorts of things. Joey asks if Mars has a stock-market, if they have computers, how they make money, etc. Finally, Caroline brings up the subject of sex. "Just how do you guys do it?" asks Caroline.

"Pretty much the way you do," responds the Martian. Discussion ensues and finally the couples decide to swap partners for the night and experience someone from a whole different dimension. Caroline and the male Martian go off to a bedroom where the Martian strips. She is shocked at what she sees. His member is teeny, tiny—about half an inch long and just a quarter inch thick.

I don't think this is going to work," says Caroline. "Why?" he asks, "What's the matter?" "Well," she replies, "It's just not long enough or big enough. I just don't see how we can do it."

"No problem," the Martian says. He proceeds to slap his forehead with his palm. With each slap of his forehead, his member grows until it becomes very long.

"Well," she says, "That's is damn impressive, but it's still pretty narrow..." "No problem," he says, and starts pulling his ears. With each pull, his member grows wider and wider until it is huge which is extremely exciting to Caroline.

"Wow!" she exclaims, as they fell into bed and made wild, crazy sex.

The next day the couples rejoin their normal partners and go their separate ways. As they walk along, Joey asks "Well, was it any good?" "I have to say," says Caroline, "it was pretty wonderful. How about you?"

"It was horrible," he replies. "All I got was a headache. All she kept doing the whole time was slapping my forehead and pulling my ears."

As odd as someone's actions may seem to you it is quite possible that they are normal and purposeful to them.

A Misinterpretation

One day Mr. O'Reilly, the president of a large corporation, called his vice-president, Tom, into his office and said, "Tom, we're making some cutbacks, so either Jack or Maddy will have to be laid off. I need you to make the decision by the end of the week."

Tom looked at Mr. O'Reilly and said, "Maddy is my best worker, but Jack has a wife and three kids. I don't know who I should to fire."

The next morning Tom waited for his employees to arrive. Maddy was the first to come in, so Tom called her in and said, "Maddy, I've got a problem. You see, I've got to either lay you or Jack off and I don't know what to do?"

Maddy replied, "You'd better jack off. I didn't sleep well and I have a headache."

Be very clear about what action you are about to do—especially in today's easily offended culture.

The Accusation

The lady of the house was convinced the maid was stealing her underwear. After she lost her third pair in a week she set up a meeting with the maid. She waited for her husband to come home and then called a meeting with the maid. She immediately accused the maid of stealing her underwear.

The Maid was flabbergasted and immediately turned to the husband and said, "Sir, you are my witness, you know I never wear panties."

Prepare yourself—you never know what is going to come up in a meeting.

Proud Mothers

Four Catholics ladies are having coffee together. The first one proudly tells her friends, "My son is a priest. When he walks into a room, everyone calls him 'Father'"

The second woman boastfully chirps, "My son is a Bishop. Whenever he walks into a room, people say, 'Your Grace.'"

The third woman says braggingly, "My son is a Cardinal. Whenever he walks into a room, people say, 'Your Eminence.'"

The fourth woman sips her coffee in silence. The first three women give her this subtle "Well.....?" She replies, "My son is a gorgeous, 6'4, hard bodied stripper. When he walks into a room, people say, 'Oh my God!'"

It is far more impressive when others discover your good qualities without your help. What kills a skunk is the publicity it gives itself.

Southern Interpretation

A man passing through a small town in the south during the holidays came across a huge nativity scene. The exhibit was impressive and he could tell that great skill and talent had gone into creating it.

However, there was one feature that bothered the man— the three wise men were all wearing fireman's helmets. Totally unable to come up with a reason for explanation, the man left.

Stopping for gas at local convenient store, the man asked the lady behind the counter about the helmets. She exploded into a rage, yelling at the man, "You Damn Yankees never do read the Bible!"

Puzzled and somewhat afraid, the man assured the lady that he does read the Bible but simply could not recall anything about firemen. She jerked her Bible from behind the counter and sticking her finger in his face she said, "It plainly says in this here good book that the three wise men came from afar.'"

Every culture has its own vocabulary. Do our best to familiarize yourself so your communication doesn't get lost in translation.

Goat Soup

Once, a villager owned a donkey and a goat. He used the donkey to carry loads of articles from the village to the city where he would roam around the whole day selling his articles. Sometime he could lend his donkey to others on hire when they needed it. As the donkey worked hard the whole day, the villager used to feed the donkey more food than he gave to the goat.

The goat became very jealous of the donkey. He advised the donkey, "You work all day long and hardly get any rest. You must act that you are sick and fall down unconscious. This way, you'll get rest for a few days."

The donkey agreed to this and acted as if he was ill. The villager called the doctor. The doctor said, "Your donkey has a strange illness. To cure him, you must feed him the soup made of a goat's lungs."

The villager at once killed the goat and cooked soup out of his lungs. Then he fed the soup to the donkey.

Advice given out of jealousy will cook you!

Birthday Certificate

There is a fellow who is talking to his buddy and says, "I don't know what to get my wife for her birthday. She has everything, and besides, she can afford to buy anything she wants. I'm stumped."

His buddy says, "I have an idea. Why don't you make up a certificate that says she can have two hours of great sex, any way she wants it. She'll probably be thrilled!"

The first fellow does just that. The next day, his buddy asks, "Well, did you take my suggestion? How did it turn out?"

"She loved it. She jumped up, thanked me, kissed me on the mouth, and ran out the door yelling, 'I'll see you in two hours!'"

The best laid plans often don't turn out as we plan.

The Helicopter Ride

Walter took his wife Ethel to the state fair every year, and every time he would say to her, "Ethel, you know that I'd love to go for a ride in that helicopter."

But Ethel would always reply, "I know that Walter, but that helicopter ride is 50 dollars and 50 dollars is 50 dollars."

Finally, they went to the fair, and Walter said to Ethel, "Ethel, you know I'm 87 years old now. If I don't ride that helicopter this year, I may never get another chance."

Once again Ethel replied, "Walter, you know that helicopter is 50 dollars and 50 dollars is 50 dollars."

The helicopter pilot overheard the couple's conversation and said, "Listen folks, I'll make a deal with you. I'll take both of you for a ride; if you can both stay quiet for the entire ride and not say a word I won't charge you! But if you say just one word, it's 50 dollars."

Walter and Ethel agreed and up they went in the helicopter. The pilot performed all kinds of fancy moves and tricks, but not a word was said by either Walter or Ethel. The pilot did his death-defying tricks over and over again, but still there wasn't so much as one word said.

When they finally landed, the pilot turned to Walter and said, "Wow! I've got to hand it to you. I did everything I could to get you to scream or shout out, but you didn't. I'm really impressed!"

Walter replied, "Well to be honest I almost said something when Ethel fell out but, you know, 50 dollars is 50 dollars!"

There is a price to pay if you talk when you have been told not to.

The Psychic Daughter

Bill is putting his young daughter to bed one night and as he walks out the bedroom door he hears her saying her prayers. She says, "God bless mommy, daddy, and grandma, rest in peace grandpa." Bill rushes back into her bedroom and asks her, "Why did you say the last part?" His daughter replies, "Because I needed to." The next day, grandpa died. Bill is worried about his daughter but thinks, it must just be a sad coincidence.

That night he tucks his daughter into bed again and once again he hears her saying her prayers. She says, "God bless mommy and daddy, rest in peace grandma." Bill is now really worried and thinking to himself, "Can my daughter really see into the future?" The next day, grandma dies and now Bill is convinced his daughter can predict the future.

For the rest of the week nothing happens, but on the Sunday night as Bill leaves his daughter's bedroom he waits outside and listens for any more prayers. Sure enough, he hears her say, "God bless you mommy, rest in peace daddy." Now Bill is really panicking and thinking, "'Oh God, I'm going to die tomorrow!"

The following day Bill is in a complete mess all day in work; a real nervous wreck. He constantly checks the clock, looks around the room and is on edge all the time expecting to die at any moment. He is so nervous that he doesn't leave the office until it's past midnight. Once it turns midnight he says to himself with relief, "How is this possible? I should be dead!" He goes home and walks into the house to find his wife sitting on the sofa with a scared look on her face. She asks him, "Where have you been? What took you so long?"

Bill replies, "Listen honey, today I haven't had the best of days" and he is just about to tell her what has happened when she starts crying and bursts out, "Our gardener died yesterday!"

It helps to know all the facts when making predictions.

The Interview

Reporter: "Excuse me, may I interview you?"

Man: "Yes!"

Reporter: "Name?"

Man: "Billy Bob"

Reporter: "Sex?"

Man: "Three to five times a week."

Reporter: "No no! I mean male or female?"

Man: "Yes, male, female... sometimes camel."

Reporter: "Holy cow!"

Man: "Yes, cow, sheep... animals in general."

Reporter: "But isn't that hostile?"

Man: "Yes, horse style, dog style, any style."

Reporter: "Oh dear!"

Man: "No, no deer. Deer run too fast. Hard to catch."

Questions are all about interpretation.

Eleven Marriages

A lawyer married a woman who had previously divorced 10 husbands. On their wedding night, she told her new husband, "Please be gentle, I'm still a virgin." "What?" said the puzzled groom. "How can that be if you've been married 10 times?"

"Well, Husband No.1 was a sales representative. He kept telling me how great it was going to be.

Husband No.2 was in software services. He was never really sure how it was supposed to function, but he said he'd look into it and get back to me.

Husband No.3 was from field services. He said everything checked out diagnostically, but he just couldn't get the system up.

Husband No.4 was in telemarketing. Even though he knew he had the order, he didn't know when he would be able to deliver.

Husband No.5 was an engineer. He understood the basic process, but wanted three years to research, implement, and design a new state-of-the-art method.

Husband No.6 was from finance and administration. He thought he knew how, but he wasn't sure whether it was his job or not.

Husband No.7 was in marketing. Although he had a nice product, he was never sure how to position it.

Husband No.8 was a psychologist. All he ever did was talk about it.

Husband No.9 was a gynecologist. All he did was look at it.

Husband No.10 was a stamp collector. All he ever did was—well you can use your imagination. God, I miss him!

"But now that I've married you, I'm really excited!"

"Good," said the new husband, "but, why?"

"You're a lawyer. This time I know I'm going to get screwed!"

Every profession carries with it its own set of preconceived perceptions.

A Rough Day

There was this guy at a bar, just looking at his drink. He stays like that for a half hour. Then a big trouble-making truck driver steps next to him, takes the drink from the guy, and just drinks it all down.

The poor man starts crying. The truck driver says, "Come on man, I was just joking. Here, I'll buy you another drink. I just can't stand to see a grown man cry."

"No, it's not that," the man replies, wiping his tears, "This day is the worst of my life. First, I oversleep and I go in late to my office. My outraged boss fires me. When I leave the building to go to my car, I find out it was stolen. The police say they can do nothing. I get a cab to go home, and when I get out, I remember I left my wallet. The cab driver just drives away. I go inside my house where I find my wife in bed with the gardener. I leave my home, come to this bar, and just when I was thinking about putting an end to my life, you show up and drink my poison."

Pranks, no matter how seemingly harmless, can backfire!

The Situation

You are on a horse, galloping at a constant speed. On your right side is a sharp drop off, and on your left side is an elephant traveling at the same speed as you. Directly in front of you is another galloping horse but your horse is unable to overtake it. Behind you is a lion running at the same speed as you and the horse in front of you. What must you do to safely get out of this highly dangerous situation?

Get your drunk self off the merry-go-round!

FEAR=False Evidence Appearing Real.

Buddha's Walk

Once Buddha was walking from one town to another town with a few of his followers. This was in the initial days. While they were traveling, they happened to pass a lake. They stopped there and Buddha told one of his disciples, "I am thirsty. Please get me some water from that lake there".

The disciple walked up to the lake. When he reached it, he noticed that some people were washing clothes in the water and, right at that moment, a bullock cart started crossing the lake right at the edge of it. As a result, the water became very muddy, very turbid. The disciple thought, "How can I give this muddy water to Buddha to drink?!" So he came back and told the Buddha, "The water in there is very muddy. I don't think it is fit to drink".

So, the Buddha said, let us take a little rest here by the tree. After about half an hour, again Buddha asked the same disciple to go back to the lake and get him some water to drink. The disciple obediently went back to the lake. This time he found that the lake had absolutely clear water in it. The mud had settled down and the water above it looked fit to be had. So he collected some water in a pot and brought it to the Buddha.

The Buddha looked at the water, and then he looked up at the disciple and said, "See, You let the water be and the mud settled down on its own. You got a clear water. It didn't require any effort".

Your mind is also like that. When it is disturbed, just let it be. Give it a little time. It will settle down on its own. You don't have to put in any effort to calm it down. We can judge and make our best decisions of our life when we stay calm.

The Smartest Man In The World

A doctor, a lawyer, a little boy and a priest were out for a Sunday afternoon flight on a small private plane. Suddenly, the plane developed engine trouble. In spite of the best efforts of the pilot, the plane started to go down. Finally, the pilot grabbed a parachute and yelled to the passengers that they better jump, and he himself bailed out

Unfortunately, there were only three parachutes remaining.

The doctor grabbed one and said "I'm a doctor, I save lives, so I must live," and jumped out.

The lawyer then said, "I'm a lawyer and lawyers are the smartest people in the world. I deserve to live." He grabbed the pack off the boy's back and jumped.

The priest looked at the little boy and said, "My son, I've lived a long and full life. You are young and have your whole life ahead of you. Take the last parachute and live in peace."

The little boy handed the parachute back to the priest and said, "Not to worry Father. The smartest man in the world just took off with my back pack."

Supposed smart people don't always make smart choices.

My Humps

A mother camel and a baby camel were lying around, and suddenly the baby camel asked, "mother, may I ask you some questions? The mother said, "Sure! Why son, is there something bothering you? Baby said, "Why do camels have humps?" The mother said, "Well son, we are desert animals, we need the humps to store water and we are known to survive without water".

Baby said, "Okay, then why are our legs long and our feet rounded?" The mother said, "Son, obviously they are meant for walking in the desert. You know with these legs I can move around the desert better than anyone does!" Baby said, "Okay, then why are our eyelashes long? Sometimes it bothers my sight". Mother with pride said, "My son, those long thick eyelashes are your protective cover. They help to protect your eyes from the desert sand and wind".

Baby after thinking said, "I see. So the hump is to store water when we are in the desert, the legs are for walking through the desert and these eyelashes protect my eyes from the desert than what in God's name are we doing here in the Zoo!?"

The bottom line is you are born with all you the things you need to be successful. The important thing is to not lock them away but put yourself in places where you can use them!

Learn From The Colonel

Once, there was an older man, who was broke, living in a tiny house and owned a beat up car. He was living off of 99 dollars social security checks. At 65 years of age, he decide things had to change. So he thought about what he had to offer. His friends raved about his chicken recipe. He decided that this was his best shot at making a change.

He left Kentucky and traveled to different states to try to sell his recipe. He told restaurant owners that he had a mouthwatering chicken recipe. He offered the recipe to them for free, just asking for a small percentage on the items sold. Sounds like a good deal, right?

Unfortunately, not to most of the restaurants. He heard NO over 1000 times. Even after all of those rejections, he didn't give up. He believed his chicken recipe was something special. He got rejected 1009 times before he heard his first yes.

With that one success Colonel Hartland Sanders changed the way Americans eat chicken. Kentucky Fried Chicken, popularly known as KFC, was born.

Remember, never give up and always believe in yourself in spite of rejection.

A Valuable Lesson

A popular speaker started off a seminar by holding up a 20 dollar bill. A crowd of 200 had gathered to hear him speak. He asked, "Who would like this 20 dollar bill?"

Two hundred hands went up.

He said, "I am going to give this 20 dollars bill to one of you but first, let me do this." He crumpled the bill up.

He then asked, "Who still wants it?"

All two hundred hands were still raised.

"Well," he replied, "What if I do this?" Then he dropped the bill on the ground and stomped on it with his shoes.

He picked it up, and showed it to the crowd. The bill was all crumpled and dirty.

"Now who still wants it?"

All the hands still went up.

"My friends, I have just showed you a very important lesson. No matter what I did to the money, you still wanted it because it did not decrease in value. It was still worth 20 dollars. Many times in our lives, life crumples us and grinds us into the dirt. We make bad decisions or deal with poor circumstances. We feel worthless. But no matter what has happened or what will happen, you will never lose your value. You are special—don't ever forget it!"

The Boss's Advice

In the morning Tom places a calls to his boss:

"Good morning, boss, unfortunately I'm not coming to work today. I'm really sick. I got a headache, stomach ache, and my both hands and legs hurt, so I'm not coming into work."

The boss replies: "You know Tom, I really need you today. When I feel like this I go to my wife, and tell her to give me sex. That makes me feel better, and I can go to work. You should try that."

Two hours later Bob calls back:

"Boss, I followed your advice, and I feel great! I'll be at work soon. By the way, you've got a really nice house!"

Be very clear when giving advice.

Enlightening

A man and woman had been married for 30 years, and in those 30 years, they always had sex in the darkest of rooms. They never even saw each other naked.

The man was embarrassed by his size and was so scared that he couldn't please her. So, from the very first time he always used a large sex toy on her. All these years she had no clue.

One day, after discovering her wild side, she decided to reach over and turn the light switch on and saw that he was using a massive sex toy.

She yelled out "I knew it, asshole, explain the sex toy!" He said, "Explain the children!"

Shedding light on some things may lead to having to answer some hard questions.

The Cowboy Prisoner

A cowboy was taken prisoner by a bunch of angry group of Natives who appeared to be celebrating. They were all prepared to kill him but their Chief declared that since they were celebrating the Great Spirit, they would grant the cowboy three wishes before killing him. The cowboy can do nothing, but obey them.

The Chief comes up to him and asks, "What do you want for your first wish?" "I want talk to my horse," replies the cowboy.

The Chief allows him to talk to the horse. The cowboy whispers in its ear. The horse neighs, rears back, and takes off at full speed. About an hour later, the horse comes back with a beautiful naked lady on its back. Well, the Tribe is very impressed, so they let the cowboy use one of their teepees. A little while later, the cowboy stumbles out of the teepee, tucking in his shirt.

The Chief asks him once again, "What do you want for your second wish?" "I want to talk to my horse, once again" replies the cowboy.

Again, the cowboy whispers in the horse's ear. The horse neighs, rears back, and takes off at full speed. About an hour later, the horse comes back with another beautiful naked lady on its back. Well, the Tribe is very impressed indeed. So, once again, they let the cowboy use one of their teepees. The cowboy stumbles out a little while later.

The chief comes up to the cowboy and asks, "So, what do you want for your last third wish?" "I want to talk to my horse, for the third time," replies the cowboy.

He grabs the horse by the ears and yells in its ear, "Can't you hear? I said POSSE, P.O.S.S.E.

Sometimes you have to spell out exactly what you mean when giving instructions.

The Builder

As I walked through my hometown.
I saw a group of men tearing a building down.

With a heave and a ho and a mighty yell,
They swung a beam and the stairway fell.

And I said to the foreman, "Are these men skilled,
The type you'd hire if you wanted to build?"

And he laughed and said, "Why no indeed."
He said, "Common labor's all I need."

"For I can tear down in a day or two."
"What it took a builder ten years to do."

And I thought to myself as I walked away,
Which of these roles am I going to play?

Am I the type that constantly tears down
As I make my way, foolishly, around?

Or am I the type that's trying to build with care,
In hopes that my team will be glad I'm there?"

Hold The Rope

Every year a professional team wins the championship. Every year a college team wins the NCAA title. Every year the best high school team in each division wins a state championship All these teams have one thing in common—no matter how tough it became throughout their season, they did one thing—they held the rope!

What is holding the rope? Imagine that you are hanging from the edge of a cliff with a drop of twenty thousand feet. The only thing between you and an fall to your death is a rope, with the person of your choice on the other end. Who do you know that has the guts to pull you to safety?

Who will hold the rope? Who do you know that is going to let that rope burn their hand and not let go? How many people that you know are going to withstand the burning pain and watch the blood drip from their hands for you?

If you can name two people, that's not good enough, because those two people might not be around. The next time your team is together, look around and ask yourself, "Who could I trust to hold the rope? Who is going to let their hands bleed for me?"

When you can look at every member on your team and say to yourself that they all would hold the rope, you are destined to win a lot of games. You see, the team that holds the rope when the going gets tough are winners. When you are down by four points with thirty seconds to go, don't give up. Yell at your teammates to "hold the rope — let it burn but don't let go!" Every year there are winners and losers in all sports. Every year the winners hold the rope. You don't have to have the best team on the field to win the game. If you play with poise and do what your coaches ask of you, and most of all — hold the rope — you will be successful. No matter what sport you play, in order to win, you have to have a commitment to your team. If you are supposed to run three times per week, do it.

If you have to lift weights three times per week, don't miss. Once you start letting up at practice or start missing your workouts, you've killed the team because you didn't hold the rope! Don't let your team down! You've got to hold the rope!

The Greatest Story Ever Told

Years ago, my assistant gave me a book for Christmas. When I saw the title, *The Greatest Story Ever Told,* I opened the book with great excitement, because I wanted to learn what it was about. But all I saw were blank pages. Inside was a note from my assistant that said, Your life is before you. Fill these pages with kind acts, good thoughts, and matters of your heart. Write a great story with your life."

We really do have the power to write our own story.

Do You Know Their Name?

A business executive by the name of Walt Bettinger likes to tell the story of the only course in college in which he failed to get an A. Bettinger, the president and CEO of the Charles Schwab Corporation, was in his senior year and really determined to keep his perfect 4.0 grade-point average. He had spent hours studying and memorizing formulas for a different upper-level business course.

The professor handed out the final exam and it was on just one piece of paper, which surprised everyone because they had anticipated a test with dozens of questions, as Bettinger recalled in an interview with Adam Bryant, author of the Corner Office feature in the New York Times. One side of the paper was blank and when students turned it over, so was the other side.

The professor then said to them, "I've taught you everything I can teach you about business in the last ten weeks, but the most important message, the most important question, is this: What's the name of the lady who cleans this building?"

Take time to learn the names of those around you.

A Consistent Mentality

More often than not, whenever I made an error, I'd get a hit in my next at bat. If I struck out a few times, I'd be more likely to make a nice play in the field. Whatever I was struggling with, I tried to excel in another area to balance it out. I always viewed baseball as a constant internal battle within myself. You have to keep your emotions low when pressure is high, but play with passion when pressure was low. It's not about focusing on perfection so much as on consistency.

—Hall of Fame Baseball Player Cal Ripken who played in 2,632 consecutive games over more than 16 years

The Craftsman

The way to success is the way of the craftsman, where you work really hard for years. You show up every day. You do the work. You see yourself as an artist dedicated to your craft with a desire to get better every day. You put your heart and soul into your work as you strive for excellence. You desire to create perfection, knowing you'll never truly achieve it but hoping to get close to it. You try new things. You fail. You improve. You grow. You face countless challenges and tons of rejection that make you doubt yourself and cause you to want to quit. But you don't. You keep working hard, stay positive, and persevere through it all with resilience, determination, and a lot of hope and faith.

Then you make it! Everyone wants to work with you. And the world says, 'Where have you been?' And you say, 'I've been here all along, and hopefully getting better day by day.' To the world, you are an overnight success. To you, the journey continues. You're a craftsman who wants to make your next work of art your best work no matter what you have accomplished in the past.

No matter your craft always adopt the attitude of the craftsman.

And Then Some

These three little words are the secret to success. They are the difference between average people and top people in most companies.

The top people always do what is expected...and then some.

They are thoughtful of others; they are considerate and kind...and then some.

They meet their obligations and responsibilities fairly and squarely...and then some.

They are good friends and helpful neighbors...and then some.

They can be counted on in an emergency...and then some.

I am thankful for people like this, for they make the world more livable. Their spirit of service is summed up in these little words...and then some!

Peyton's Advice For Rookies

If I could give rookies a couple pieces of advice, I would start with this: 'Don't ever go to a meeting to watch a practice or a game without having already watched it by yourself.' That's one thing that I have always done. When the coach is controlling the remote control, he's gonna rewind when he wants to rewind. He's gonna skip certain plays. He's not watching every single detail. When you can control the rewind button, you can go in there and you watch—first, you better watch your mechanics. Watch what you're doing. Is your drop good? How's your throw? OK, now rewind it again. Now you better watch your receivers. OK, looks like Demaryius Thomas ran a good route here. Not sure what Julius Thomas was doing here. Then you better rewind it again and watch what the defense is doing. So, there's time in that deal. You have to know what they were doing so you can help them. So that has helped me. When I go in and watch it with the coach, I'm watching it for the third, fourth, fifth time. That's when you start learning.

—*Peyton Manning*

The Dream Team

The following comes from Chuck Daly's first team meeting with the 1992 Olympic "Dream Team." But first, let's just review the Dream Team roster: Charles Barkley, Larry Bird, Clyde Drexler, Patrick Ewing, Magic Johnson, Michael Jordan, Christian Laettner, Karl Malone, Chris Mullen, Scottie Pippen, David Robinson, and John Stockton.

At a early team meeting, Coach Daly approached the most delicate subject, "Look, there are twelve of you, and you are all All-Stars and future Hall of Famers," said Daly. "and there is no way I can get all of the minutes you're use to having on....Magic and Jordan interrupted him.

"That isn't going to be a problem," said Jordan.

"We're here to win, and nobody is going to care about playing time, Chuck," Magic said.

Such problems, particularly the knotty one of minutes, are rarely solved that easily. This one was. Magic and Jordan said there would not be a problem, and that was that.

Barbers Don't Exist

A man went to a barber-shop to have his hair and his beard cut as always. He started to have a good conversation with the barber who attended him. They talked about various things and various subjects. Suddenly, they touched the subject of God.

The barber said: "Look man, I don't believe that God exists as you say."

"Why do you say that?" asked the client.

"Well, it's so easy, you just have to go out in the street to realize that God does not exist. Oh, tell me, if God existed, would there be so many sick people? Would there be abandoned children? If God existed, there would be no suffering nor pain. I can't think of a loving a God who permits all of these things."

The client stopped for a moment, thinking, but he didn't want to respond so as to cause an argument.

The barber finished his job and the client went out of the shop. Just as he got out of the barbershop he saw a man in the street with long and unkempt hair and beard—it looked like it had been a long time since he had his cut, and he looked so untidy.

The client quickly went back inside the barber shop again and he said to the barber, "You know what? Barbers do not exist."

"How can you say they don't exist?" asked the barber. "I am a barber and here I am, I exist!"

"No!" the client exclaimed. "They don't exist because if they did there would be no people with long hair and beard like that man on the street."

"Ah, barbers do exist, what happens is that people do not come to me."

"Exactly!" affirmed the client. "That's the point. God does exist, what happens is people don't go to Him and do not look for Him."

Faith is knowing that you know without having seen what you know.

Slow Down

A young and successful executive was traveling down a neighborhood street, going a bit too fast in his new Jaguar. He was watching for kids darting out from between parked cars and slowed down when he thought he saw something. As his car passed, no children appeared. Instead, a brick smashed into the Jag's side door!

He slammed on the brakes and backed the Jag back to the spot where the brick had been thrown. The angry driver then jumped out of the car, grabbed the nearest kid and pushed him up against a parked car shouting, "What the hell was that all about and who are you? What are you doing? That's a new car and that brick you threw is going to cost a lot of money. Why did you do it?"

The young boy was apologetic. "Please, mister...please! I'm sorry but I didn't know what else to do," he pleaded. "I threw the brick because no one else would stop!" With tears dripping down his face and off his chin, the youth pointed to a spot just around a parked car. "It's my brother," he said. "He rolled off the curb and fell out of his wheelchair and I can't lift him up." Now sobbing, the boy asked the stunned executive, "Would you please help me get him back into his wheelchair? He's hurt and he's too heavy for me." Moved beyond words, the driver tried to swallow the rapidly swelling lump in his throat. He hurriedly lifted the handicapped boy back into the wheelchair, then took out a linen handkerchief and dabbed at the fresh scrapes and cuts.

A quick look told him everything was going to be okay. "Thank you and may God bless you," the grateful child told the stranger. Too shook up for words, the man simply watched the boy push his wheelchair-bound brother down the sidewalk toward their home.

It was a long, slow walk back to the Jaguar. The damage was very noticeable, but the driver never bothered to repair the dented side door. He kept the dent there to remind him of this message

Don't go through life so fast that someone has to throw a brick at you to get your attention!

Tricky Jar

An 85-year-old man goes to see his doctor for his regular physical exam. The doctor says that the man needs to provide a semen sample and gives him a jar saying, "Take this jar home with you and come back tomorrow with a semen sample."

The next day the old man goes back to the doctors and gives him the jar, which is as clean and empty as when the doctor gave it to him. So the doctor asks what happened and why there is no sperm sample in the jar. The old man says, "Well, doc, it's like this... first I tried with my right hand, but nothing. Then I tried with my left hand, but still nothing. Then I asked my wife for help. She tried with her right hand - nothing; then with her left, still nothing. She tried with her mouth, first with the teeth in, then with her teeth out, still nothing. We even called up Mary, the nice lady next door and she tried too, first with both hands, then an armpit, and she even tried squeezing it between her knees, but still nothing."

The doctor is really shocked by all this and asks incredulously, "You asked your neighbor?"

The old man replies, "Yep, not one of us could get the jar open."

Your mind can create all sorts of scenarios when you jump to conclusions.

Speeding Motorist

Late one night this guy is speeding down the empty road. A cop sees him go flying past so chases him and pulls him over. The cop goes up to the car and when the man rolls down the window, he asks, "Are you aware of how fast you were going, sir?"

The man replies, "Yes I am. I'm trying to escape a robbery I got involved in."

The cop looks at him disbelievingly and asks him, "Were you the one being robbed, sir?"

The man casually replies, "Oh no, I was the one who committed the robbery. I was escaping."

The cop is shocked and surprised that the man has admitted this so freely. He says, "So you're telling me you were speeding...AND committed a robbery?"

"Oh yes," replies the man calmly. "I have all the loot in the back."

The cop is now starting to get angry and says, "Sir, I'm afraid you have to come with me" as he reaches into the window to take the car keys out of the ignition.

The man shouts, "Don't do that! I'm afraid that you'll find the gun in my glove compartment!" At this the cop pulls his hand out of the window and says, "Wait here" as he returns to his car and calls for backup.

Soon there are cars, cops and helicopters all over, everywhere you look. The man is quickly dragged out of his car, handcuffed and taken towards a cop car. However, just before he is put in the car and taken away a cop walks up to him and says, while pointing at the cop that pulled him over, "Sir, this officer tells us that you had committed a robbery, had stolen loot in the trunk of your car, and had a loaded gun in your glove compartment. However, we didn't find any of these things in your car."

The man replies, "Yeah, and I bet that liar said I was speeding too!"

Never be surprised at the lengths some people will go to or the things they may say to try to get out of something.

The Grieving Widow

Mary approaches Father O'Grady after mass and starts sobbing.

He says: "So what's bothering you?"

She replies: "Oh, Father, I've terrible news. My husband passed away last night."

The priest says: "Oh, Mary, that's terrible. Did he have any last requests?"

"Certainly father," she replied. "He said: "Please Mary, put down that damn gun.""

Emotion can sometimes be used to cover one's actions.

The Drunk Priest

An Irish priest is driving along a country road when a police man pulls him over. He immediately smells alcohol on the priest's breath and notices an empty wine bottle in the car.

He says: "Have you been drinking?"

"No sir! Just water," says the priest.

The cop replies: "Then why do I smell wine?"

The priest looks at the bottle and says: "Damn, Jesus has done it again!"

Don't expect a miracle to get you out of trouble.

The Burglar And The Parrot

A burglar breaks into a house in a ritzy area of town. He's sure that there's nobody home, but he still sneaks in, doesn't turn on any lights and heads straight for where he thinks the valuables are kept.

Suddenly, he hears a voice call out, "I can see you! Jesus can see you, too!"

The burglar freezes in his tracks. He doesn't move a muscle.

A couple of minutes go by. The voice repeats, "I can see you! Jesus can see you, too!"

The burglar slowly takes out his flashlight, switches it on and looks around the room. He sees a birdcage with a parrot in it.

"Did you say that?" the burglar asks the parrot.

The parrot says again, "I can see you! Jesus can see you, too!"

"Hah! So what?" says the burglar. "You're just a parrot!"

"I may be just a parrot," replies the bird, "but Jesus is a Doberman!"

Don't assume someone doesn't know what they are talking about.

A Hunting Story

Two hunters are out in the woods when one of them collapses. He doesn't seem to be breathing and his eyes are glazed.

The other guy whips out his phone and calls the emergency services. He gasps, "My friend is dead! What can I do?"

The operator says, "Calm down. I can help. First, let's make sure he's dead."

There is a silence; then a gun shot is heard. Back on the phone, the guy says, "OK, now what?"

Give very clear when giving instructions!

Snail With An Attitude

A guy is sitting at home when he hears a knock at the door. He opens the door and sees a snail on the porch. He picks up the snail and throws it as far as he can. Three years later there's a knock on the door. He opens it and sees the same snail. The snail says: 'What the hell was that all about?'

A Genie And An Idiot

Three guys stranded on a desert island find a magic lantern containing a genie, who grants them each one wish. The first guy wishes he was off the island and back home. The second guy wishes the same. The third guy says: 'I'm lonely. I wish my friends were back here.'

Real Love

It's the World Cup Final, and a man makes his way to his seat right next to the field. He sits down, noticing that the seat next to him is empty.

He leans over and asks his neighbor if someone will be sitting there. "No," says the neighbor. "The seat is empty." "This is incredible," said the man. "Who in their right mind would have a seat like this for the Final and not use it?"

The neighbor says, "Well actually the seat belongs to me. I was supposed to come with my wife, but she passed away. This is the first World Cup Final we haven't been to together since we got married.'"

"Oh, I'm so sorry to hear that. That's terrible—but couldn't you find someone else, a friend, relative or even a neighbor to take her seat?'"

The man shakes his head. "No," he says. "They're all at the funeral."

Sympathy should be reserved only for those who deserve it.

The Devil's In The Details

A guy dies and is sent to hell. Satan meets him, shows him doors to three rooms, and says he must choose one to spend eternity in. In the first room, people are standing in dirt up to their necks.

The guy says, 'No, let me see the next room.' In the second room, people are standing in dirt up to their noses. Guy says no again.

Finally Satan opens the third room. People are standing with dirt up to their knees, drinking coffee and eating pastries. The guy says, 'I pick this room.' Satan says Ok and starts to leave, and the guy wades in and starts pouring some coffee.

On the way out Satan yells, 'OK, coffee break's over. Everyone back on your heads!'

Things are not always what they appear!

Pulling Rank

One foggy night, an aircraft carrier was cruising off the coast of Newfoundland when the junior radar operator spotted a light in the gloom. Just as the radar operator realized that a collision was bound to happen he received the following radio message...

"Please divert your course at least seven degrees to the south to avoid a collision."

The junior officer replied, "You must be joking, I recommend you divert your course instead!"

He immediately referred the matter to his superior officer who reported the incident as insubordination.

The senior officer of the carrier angrily sent a second message. "I believe that I out rank you, and am giving you a direct order to divert your course now."

To which came the following reply...

"Sir, this is a lighthouse. I suggest you take evasive action, regardless of what rank you hold."

Before you start barking out orders or pulling rank it is important to know who you are talking to.

In Need Of A Push

A man and his wife were awakened at 3:00 am by a loud pounding on the door.

The man gets up and goes to the door where a drunken stranger, standing in the pouring rain, is asking for a push.

"Not a chance," says the husband, "it is 3:00 in the morning!"

He slams the door and returns to bed.

"Who was that?" asked his wife... "Just some drunk guy asking for a push," he answers.

"Did you help him?" she asks

"No, I did not, it's 3am in the morning and it's pouring rain out there!"

"Well, you have a short memory," says his wife. "Can't you remember about three months ago when we broke down, and those two guys helped us?

I think you should help him, and you should be ashamed of yourself! "God loves drunk people too you know."

The man does as he is told, gets dressed, and goes out into the pounding rain.

He calls out into the dark, "Hello, are you still there?"

"Yes," comes back the answer.

"Do you still need a push?" calls out the husband.

"Yes, please!" comes the reply from the dark.

"Where are you?" asks the husband.

"Over here... on the swing," replied the drunk.

Even your best intentions can go astray.

The Medicine Man

On his 74th birthday, a man got a gift certificate from his wife. The certificate paid for a visit to a medicine man living on a nearby reservation who was rumored to have a wonderful cure for erectile dysfunction.

After being persuaded to go, he drove to the reservation, handed his ticket to the medicine man and wondered what he was in for.

The old man handed a potion to him, and with a grip on his shoulder, warned, "This is a powerful medicine. You take only a teaspoonful and then say '1-2-3'." When you do, you will become more manly than you have ever been in your life and you can perform as long as you want."

The man was encouraged. As he walked away, he turned and asked, "How do I stop the medicine from working?"

"Your partner must say '1-2-3-4,'" the medicine man responded, "but when she does, the medicine will not work again until the next full moon."

The man was very eager to see if it worked so he went home, showered, shaved, took a spoonful of the medicine and then invited his wife to join him in the bedroom. When she came in, he quickly took off his clothes and said, "1-2-3!" Immediately, he was the manliest of men. His wife was excited and began throwing off her clothes as she asked "What was the 1-2-3 for?"

A perfect example of why we should never end our sentences with a preposition, because we could end up with a dangling participle.

The Silent Treatment

A man and his wife were having some problems at home and were giving each other the silent treatment.

Suddenly, the man realized that the next day, he would need his wife to wake him at 5:00 AM for an early morning business flight. Not wanting to be the first to break the silence—and LOSE—he wrote on a piece of paper, "Please wake me at 5:00 AM." He left it where he knew she would find it.

The next morning, the man woke up, only to discover it was 9:00 AM and he had missed his flight. Furious, he was about to go and see why his wife hadn't wakened him, when he noticed a piece of paper by the bed.

The paper said, "It is 5:00 AM. Wake up."

Sometimes it may be in your best interest to lose an argument so you can win with the important things.

Road Trip

After a heated argument, a married couple drove down a country road for several miles, not saying a word. The earlier argument had it so that neither of them wanted to concede their position.

As they passed a barnyard of mules, goats, and pigs, the husband asked sarcastically, "Relatives of yours?"

"Yep," the wife replied, "in-laws."

If you ask a smartass question you can expect a smartass answer.

The Husband Store

A store that sells husbands has just opened in New York City, where a woman may go to choose a husband. Among the instructions at the entrance is a description of how the store operates.

"You may visit the store ONLY ONCE! There are six floors and the attributes of the men increase as the shopper ascends the flights.

There is, however, a catch: you may choose any man from a particular floor, or you may choose to go up a floor, but you cannot go back down except to exit the building!"

So, a woman goes to the Husband Store to find a husband...
On the first floor the sign on the door reads: Floor 1 - These men have jobs.

The second floor sign reads: Floor 2 - These men have jobs and love kids.

The third floor sign reads: Floor 3 - These men have jobs, love kids, and are extremely good looking. "Wow," she thinks, but feels compelled to keep going.

She goes to the fourth floor and the sign reads: Floor 4 - These men have jobs, love kids, are drop-dead good looking and help with the housework.

"Oh, mercy me!" she exclaims, "I can hardly stand it!"

Still, she goes to the fifth floor and sign reads: Floor 5 - These men have jobs, love kids, are drop-dead gorgeous, help with the housework, and have a strong romantic streak.

She is so tempted to stay, but she goes to the sixth floor and the Sign reads: Floor 6 - You are visitor 31,456,012 to this floor. There are no men on this floor. This floor exists solely as proof that women are impossible to please. Thank you for shopping at the "Husband Store."

You must make a decision before you eventually run out of options.

The Wisdom of the Navajo

A woman is driving toward home in Northern Arizona when she sees a Navajo woman hitchhiking. Because the trip had been long and quiet, she stops the car and the Navajo woman climbs in.

During their small talk, the Navajo woman glances surreptitiously at a brown bag on the front seat between them. "If you're wondering what's in the bag," offers the woman, "it's a bottle of wine. I got it for my husband."

The Navajo woman is silent for a while, nods several times and says, "Good trade!"

The Marriage Counselor

A husband and wife go to a counselor after 15 years of marriage.

The counselor asks them what the problem is and the wife goes into a tirade listing every problem they have ever had in the 15 years they've been married. She goes on and on and on.

Finally, the counselor gets up, walks around the desk, embraces the wife and kisses her passionately. The woman shuts up and sits quietly in a daze.

The counselor turns to the husband and says, "This is what your wife needs at least three times a week. Can you do this?"

The husband thinks for a moment and replies, "Well, I can drop her off here on Mondays and Wednesdays, but on Fridays, I play golf."

Combine your actions with your words when trying to make a point. Actions alone are not always good indicators of the message you are trying to impart.

A Misinterpretation

How many women can a man marry?"

"Sixteen," the boy responded.

His cousin was amazed that he had an answer so quickly.

"How do you know that?"

"Easy," the little boy said.

"All you have to do is add it up, like the pastor said, 4 better, 4 worse, 4 richer, 4 poorer."

You never know how you are being interpreted.

Made Recently

A little girl was sitting on her grandfather's lap as he read her a bedtime story.

From time to time, she would take her eyes off the book and reach up to touch his wrinkled cheek.

She was alternately stroking her own cheek, then his again.

Finally she spoke up, "Grandpa, did God make you?"

"Yes, sweetheart," he answered, "God made me a long time ago"

"Oh," she paused, "Grandpa, did God make me too?"

"Yes, indeed, honey," he said, "God made you just a little while ago."

Feeling their respective faces again, she observed, "God's getting better at it, isn't he?"

We all are getting better every day!

Birthday Surprise

Last week was Chris's birthday. His wife didn't wish him a happy birthday. His parents forgot and so did his kids.

He went to work and even his colleagues didn't wish him a happy birthday. As he entered his office, his secretary said, "Happy birthday, boss!" He felt so special. She asked him out for lunch. After lunch, she invited him to her apartment.

They went there and she said, "Do you mind if I go into the bedroom for a minute?" "Okay," Chris said.

She came out five minutes later with a birthday cake, Chris's wife, his parents, his kids, his friends, and his colleagues all yelling, "SURPRISE!!!" while he was waiting on the sofa—naked.

Be very careful when making an assumption. As the old adage goes...to assume is to make an "ass" out of "u" and "me"!

Albert's Driver

A story has been told that Albert Einstein had a driver who looked very much like him—hair and all. One day he was on his way to speak at an important science conference. In route, he tells his driver, "I'm tired of all these conferences. I always say the same things over and over!"

The driver agrees: "You're right sir. As your driver, I attended every one of them, and even though I don't know anything about science, I could give the conference in your place."

"That's a great idea!" says Einstein. "Let's switch places then!" So they switch clothes and as soon as they arrive, the driver dressed as Einstein goes on stage and starts giving the usual speech, while the real Einstein, dressed as the car driver, attends it.

But in the crowd, there is one scientist who wants to impress everyone and thinks of a very difficult question to ask Einstein, hoping he won't be able to respond. So this guy stands up and interrupts the conference by posing his very difficult question. The whole room goes silent, holding their breath, waiting for the response. The driver looks at him, dead in the eye, and says "Sir, to show you how easy your question is to answer, I'm going to let my driver answer it for me."

Moral? The ability to think on your feet is more important than having all the answers!

The Last Word

Thank you for reading this collection of stories, jokes and wits of wisdom. Leading people requires enough self-confidence that you are willing to put yourself on the line. Leading requires you to have the delicate balance between not caring what some people think and caring deeply what others do. Most importantly, leading requires you to be authentic. No matter what story you tell or words you use if they are from the heart and from the real you they will be effective. If you use stories and words just to sound official or to try to fit in you can bet it won't be long until your followers begin to dwindle. One of my favorite quotes is from Carl Sagan which sums up what I'm trying to say very well....

The fact that some geniuses were laughed at does not imply that all who are laughed at are geniuses. They laughed at Columbus, they laughed at Fulton, they laughed at the Wright brothers. But they also laughed at Bozo the Clown.

Keep making a difference!

—*Dan Spainhour*

About the author

Dan Spainhour has more than 35 years of high school and college coaching experience. He has received numerous awards during his coaching career, including three state championships and nineteen coach of the year honors. His teams have collected more than 500 victories and has won nearly 70 percent of his games. In 2008, Spainhour returned to high school coaching after serving as the director of basketball operations for Florida State University. He also coached at the University of Miami where he worked under current Florida State coach, Leonard Hamilton. During his time at Miami he helped lead the Hurricanes to their first NCAA tournament appearance in 38 years. Duke's Mike Krzyzewski had this to say about Dan "It is a privilege to endorse Dan Spainhour's coaching and teaching ability. I have found him to not only be extremely knowledgeable about the game but he also has an amazing way of communicating with youngsters. It is a great combination!" While Leonard Hamilton, Florida State's basketball coach said this of Dan: "Dan Spainhour is an excellent coach. He has a tremendous understanding of the game. His teaching ability makes him one of the finest coaches in the game."

Spainhour was the founder of Educational Coaching and Business Communications, a company that later merged with The Leadership Publishing Team. He is the author of several coaching, leadership and motivational books as well as the editor of the highly acclaimed Coaching and Leadership Journal.

Leading Narratives is a product of The Leadership Publishing Team. The Leadership Publishing Team specializes in informational guidebooks, newsletters and special reports for business leaders, athletes, coaches, educators, and parents. Our Winston-Salem, North Carolina based company is committed to providing quality information and personalized service. Our mission is uncomplicated—to bring you the best guidance available in a concise, easy to understand format. Our inspirational guidebooks are being used by coaches of all sports and at every level all across the country.

Visit us at leadershippublishingteam.com.